MANCHESTER BUCCANEERS

MANCHESTER BUCCANEERS

Adrian Sherling

Weidenfeld & Nicolson
LONDON

First published in Great Britain in 2006
by Weidenfeld & Nicolson

1 3 5 7 9 10 8 6 4 2

A CIP catalogue record for this book is
available from the British Library.

ISBN-13 978 0 297 85140 0
ISBN-10 0 297 85140 3

Typeset by Deltatype Ltd,
Birkenhead, Merseyside

Printed in Great Britain by
Clays Ltd, St Ives plc

The Orion publishing group's policy is to use papers that are
natural, renewable and recyclable products and made
from wood grown in sustainable forests. The logging and
manufacturing processes are expected to conform to the
environmental regulations of the country of origin.

Weidenfeld & Nicolson

The Orion Publishing Group Ltd
Orion House
5 Upper Saint Martin's Lane
London, WC2H 9EA

www.orionbooks.co.uk

Name: Roswell P Shambling
Age: $12\frac{1}{2}$
Location: Fort Myers, FL
Occupation: I'm at school, man

 The Manchester roster

GOALTENDERS

1. Tim Howard

A giant from the US of A who is the best goaltender in the world. Drafted from the New York/New Jersey/New Republican Metrostars. Sir Ferguson likes him because they have so much in common. Both have a habit of dropping things and can't stop themselves swearing.

Eddie Vandersar

Hollandish goaltender Eddie Vandersar, who at 34 is almost as old as my Pop, played for the last four years at the Fulham Fayeds, where he gave up just 60 scores in the last series. In that time, he achieved 79 stops, batted the ball 43 times and averaged 69.4 yards per kick. He joined Manchester in a big-bucks trade with the Egyptian franchise the Fayeds for 5 million English dollars and seven camels.

DEFENSEMEN

2. Gary Neville

Our most reliable defensive back, but no good for marketing. What Manchester fan wants his name on the back of his jersey? Famous for kicking a soccer ball at an Everton Stickies fan and not knowing the words to God Save the Queen.

3. Phil Neville

See above, but delete the bit about reliability.

4. Gabriel Heinze

An Argentinia player who is one of my favourite kickers at the franchise. I love the way he runs around a lot and doesn't worry about what his hair looks like! He has so much energy, I wouldn't be surprised if he bathed in Gatorade every night. That would also explain the color of his hair I suppose.

5. Ferdinand Rio

Our Brazilian defenseman, who is being threatened with a trade if he doesn't ink a new contract at the Nike Trafford Ballpark franchise. Maybe Rio thinks he's already signed the new deal. After all, Pop tells me he even forgot to go to the bathroom once! Being a foreign person, he speaks funny and often drops letters. He drops Hs a lot, but insists he has never once dropped an E.

6. Wes Brown

Awesome kicker. He played for Britain against Team USA, so why doesn't Sir Ferguson play him more often? Pop says he looks a lot like 1980s British pop star Yazz. He has had his problems with injury, but carrying the weight of that ginger afro on his head was always going to cause problems.

22. Jono Shea

He comes from great sporting stock. His Grandpa was a baseball player for the New York Mets and was so good, they named the stadium after him. I read that whenever Shea gets the ball, fans start singing 'When Jono goes running down the wing'. These kind of aerial stunts are surely too dangerous for a soccer player.

27. Michael Silvester

Swift soccer player, who covered 40 yards in 4.55 seconds during workouts. Silvester fell out with the France head coach because he is the wrong star sign. Apparently, he is a Leo, which means he is temperamental, makes poor decisions and is a bad soccer player. You can't argue with the stars.

MIDDLEMEN

7. Cristiano Roonaldo

The older of the Roonaldo brothers currently at Manchester, he is one of our best kickers. Pop says he likes stepovers a lot, which I think is where he 'steps' around the opponent's leg and goes 'over', trying to win a 12-yard kick-ball punishment.

11. Ryan Giggs

He kicked for England youngsters, but rather unfairly, never made the step up to the senior roster. When he was younger, people talked about him in the same way they talk about the Roonaldo brothers. Now they talk about how he used to be as good as the Roonaldo brothers.

16. Roy Keano

My favorite player, but I can't understand why he hasn't played for England. He is fierce in ball-gaining situations and is the offensive captain of the side. One bad point though is the time Pop tells me he tried to hurt his own Manchester team-mate Alf Haaland in the middle of a game.

17. Liam Miller

Added on a no-English dollar relocation fee from the Glasgow-Ireland Greens. I know nothing else about him. I'm not sure he ever played for Manchester or is still there. The last time anyone saw him, he was reading a book by the magician David Copperfield about how to reverse the trick to make you invisible.

18. Paul Scholes

The best red-haired player ever to kick for Manchester in their 13-year history. Scholes was one of the best score-kicking middlemen in the EPL, as his tally of 128 scores for Manchester proves. His tally of nine scores in 18 months proves that he is no longer one of the top score-kicking middlemen around.

25. Quinton Fortune

A kicker from Southern Africa who only plays when better kickers are on the Injured Reserve. He probably has the highest pay-per-kick ratio for the franchise, considering he kicks very, very little.

31. Darren Fletcher

The new Roy Keano, and he's not been picked for England either. Sir Ferguson always talks about how good the young players are at Nike Trafford Ballpark, by saying, 'We've got a great set of youngsters here at Manchester. Wayne and Cristiano are going to be two of the best players in the world soon. And Darren Fletcher is young as well.'

OFFENSERS

8. Wayne Roonaldo

The younger of the Roonaldo brothers and he is a genius. I hope he is going to help Manchester get over their no-scoring streaks this year. Pop tells me Roonaldo scores a lot, especially with the grandmas.

9. Lewis Saha

Manchester traded Saha for over 20 million English dollars from the Fulham Fayeds and he repaid them with two scores last series. Saha is even quicker than Silvester, clocking 4.45 for the 40-yard sprint in summer camp workouts.

10. Rude Nistelrooy

Rude Nistelrooy, whose nickname is The Van due to his poor turning circle, has committed to Manchester for another series, despite interest from Portugalese club Realmadrid. He is our top offenser, as his six EPL scores last series clearly show.

12. David Bellion

Sir Ferguson traded him thinking he would be Manchester's version of Thierry Henry, but the only similairty is that he is French and now kicks for a London franchise. As fast as Maurice Green, but about as good at kicking as him as well.

14. Alan Smith

A great player, as shown by him being picked to play for England. Pop says he plays with his heart on his sleeve, which seems a bit dangerous to me.

 May 15 — The Glazers are coming!

When I was young, Malcolm Glazer bought my local NFL team, the Tampa Bay Buccaneers. We were an average, mid-division franchise with little hope of any championship games.

Yet when Glazer took over, he and his money rejuvenated the team, and within a few years we were the world champions. We owe all of that to the business skill of Malcolm Glazer (although the players may have had a part to play as well).

Now I see that Glazer has bought EPL soccer roster Manchester and although I don't know a whole lot about soccer, I am going to start rooting for Manchester now.

They are a mid-division franchise in a similar position to the one Tampa Bay were in, having finished only third in the standings last series. But I'm confident that, with the Glaz-meister in charge, they can also become world champions sometime.

I'm going to have to learn about soccer as I go along, but here's what I have managed to pick up so far from my Pop:

1) All the best soccer kickers have off-the-gridiron problems:

    George Best = drank too much
    Maradona = ate too much
    Paul Gazza = drank *and* ate too much
    Pelé = erectile dysfunction

2) Brazil is the current world champion nation, having won the last World Cup. I can't wait for the next one. I'm going to start watching the World Cup every year.
3) The London Chelseas are the current EPL champion franchise, winning the pennant with games to spare. Just last week, they destroyed Manchester three to one at the Trafford Ballpark, proving how far behind we are.
4) Manchester face a really tough task to rise up the divisional standings. The London Chelseas are loaded after being bought by Russia. And today I read a headline that read, 'North Korea boosts Arsenal.'

May 16 — Manchester fans hail Glazer's arrival

Manchester fans have crowded the streets around the Trafford Ballpark to celebrate the new dawn at the franchise.

Many fans made models of the American billionaire and it was incredibly unfortunate that they all somehow managed to catch fire. Too many people must have been smoking cigarettes.

They were all chanting 'Not for sale', which is true, as the franchise is no longer for sale now that Glazer has taken it off the Wall Street market.

There were also banners saying 'RIP Glazer', I wasn't sure what they meant, so I asked Pop and he says that in London, where Manchester plays, rip is a word that means great. As in:

'Was it a good score?'

'Yes, it was a ripper.'

He says former Manchester goaltender Mark Bosnich brought the word into everyday use, having heard it on a TV show called *Neighbours*.

May 17 — The South Hamptons 1—2 Manchester

The Malcolm Glazer era at Manchester got off to the winningest of starts Sunday with an overtaking EPL victory over the South Hamptons in the final regulation game of the current series.

We had been facing an embarrassing no-pointer when left cornerback Jono Shea hit a negative score after goaltender Roy Carroll batted the ball in the six-yard zone.

But Shea made up for his error with an assist, crossing the ball for Darren Fletcher who head-kicked home, threatening to take the game into overtime.

The South Hamptons needed a draw and for nearest rivals the Western Bromwiches and Crystal Palisades to lose to remain in the EPL next series and after 62 minutes, things were looking good. After 63 however, a silence descended over the HMS St Mary's.

First, both the Palisades and Bromwiches kicked scores, then the Hamptons lost one themselves. Rude Nistelrooy got the all-important come-from-behind point-getter, bundling Alan Smith's ricocheted center into the scoring zone. It was enough to ensure the win and guarantee that Manchester fans took Glazer to their hearts.

The regular-time end-score means that the Hamptons picked up one of the lowest three spots in the standings and were demoted. They must play AAA minor league soccer next season, having previously been in the EPL since soccer was invented in 1992.

Meanwhile, the win guaranteed Manchester third position in the standings, which is the joint highest we've finished for ages.

May 18 — The Nevilles are coming!

I've just found out that Britain are playing Team USA at soccer in Chicago next week! And four Manchester players will be there!

8

This is so cool, because it's the first time I can watch some of Manchester's star players like Phil Neville and Gary Neville and Wes Brown and Alan Smith.

Alan Smith is unbelievable, overcoming the handicap of an appalling hairstyle to live a normal everyday life. And he got 10 scores in one season! I feel sorry for Team USA goaltender Timmy Howard. Smith's gonna rock his world, probably by charging in on him, long after he caught the ball.

Of course Team USA are no pushovers nowadays and are actually ranked above Britain in the world rankings. And after convincing wins over Honduras and Guatemala, who could doubt that?

May 19 – The Super Bowl of Soccer

It's the Super Bowl of Soccer Saturday when my mighty Manchester takes on the London Arsenals in the western England city of Wales.

It's called the SA Super Bowl and has a long history going even beyond the start of division football in Britain in 1992. I read that Manchester won it last year with a three-zip win over the Millwall Mods. Now all the players have winners' rings, they shouldn't have any nerves and will win easily this year. It would be great if Glazer could start his time at Manchester with a pennant win.

The SA Super Bowl is in a play-off format with a no-strike rule, meaning you lose, you're outta there! Manchester and the London Arsenals are the only two teams with a 100% record in the competition.

In fact, the London Arsenals are the dominant franchise in this pennant, lifting the Bowl two out of the last three years, even beating the London Chelseas in one of the finals.

The London Arsenals' head coach is called Arsene Wenger. What kind of dumb name is that? I think he is a foreigner, which is strange as the Arsenals are English. At least Manchester's head coach has got a totally English name. He

is called Sir Alex Ferguson. You don't get more English than
that.

May 20 — Glazer — what a businessman!

Malcolm Glazer gets better by the day! I've loved him ever
since he turned my beloved Buccs into Super Bowl
champions, but his work in his short time with Manchester
soccer roster is nothing short of awesome!

I read that he is thinking of changing the name of the
arena Manchester play in. At the moment, it's
called the Trafford Ballpark, which is so dull.
The Nike Trafford Ballpark is a much better
name and helps get some money in. After all, I
noticed that Manchester is in a great deal of
debt nowadays.

There are also rumors that he could create more franchises
of Manchester, bringing one to the Major League Soccer
pennant in the US. I'd love to see the Tampa Bay
Manchesters competing against some of the other incredible
teams over here like Real Salt Lake, Atletico Baltimore and
the Detroit Spinners.

I think he is also going to introduce cheerleaders to
Manchester. It wouldn't be the first time though . . . a long
time ago, they had a set of cheerleaders called the Busby
Babes, but Pop tells me they weren't the best-looking bunch!

It's great to see Malcolm already working his magic. Soon
Manchester will be a team famous worldwide, not just in
the south of England!

May 21 — Introducing the London Arsenals

Manchester faces the biggest encounter of their series as
they take on the London Arsenals in the SA Super Bowl. We
have beaten them twice already this series and yet somehow
they still managed to grab a spot ahead of us in the EPL
standings.

So who are the kickers we will be up against tomorrow? I'm still new to this soccer, so with the help of my Pop, I will attempt to talk you through our opponents.

Jens Lehmann

Germanish goaltender for whom the word fruitcake was invented. In his two years at the Arsenals, he has been banned for throwing the ball at someone and spraying a referee with water. Next series, I expect him to moon at a line judge and flick an opponent's ear with a ruler.

Gail Clichy, Lauren

The London Arsenals, coming from the British capital city, are a very cosmopolitan bunch and as well as having a large number of foreign players, they also are the only franchise to feature two lady kickers.

Ashley Cole

Britain star Ashley Cole was caught with the General Manager of the London Chelseas doing something naughty earlier this series. All the British websites are talking about tapping up, although in America, we don't have taps, we have faucets. I have no idea why a top soccer player was putting new faucets up. Maybe Cole isn't getting paid enough, if he has to do plumbing jobs in his spare time. Pop says plumbers in Britain are millionaires.

Gilbert O'Silva

Irish Middleman who Pop says 'plugs the hole'. No wonder the London Arsenals need Cole to come round and unblock them again.

May 22 — Manchester 0–0 London Arsenals

The London Arsenals are the SA Super Bowl champions after winning a 12-yeard kick-ball challenge against Manchester after the game finished as a zip-zip tie.

Manchester kicked much better than their local rivals in the game, but could not hit a slap shot score when it mattered.

Wayne Roonaldo came closest when he hit the metalwork with a shot/cross, while Rude Nistelrooy thought he had got the win when he head-kicked a corner ball from the two-yard line, but he aimed it straight at a London Arsenals player on the scoreline. So unlucky!

When Arsenals star Antonio Jose Reyes was given a naughty ejection by the referee, Manchester had a whole minute to make their superiority count, but were unable to find a way through the Arsenals' D.

As no one could break the tie, the referee decided they would all shoot from the 12-yard kick spot until someone didn't score. Unfortunately, Paul Scholes kicked the ball and it hit the London goaltender and Manchester had lost the SA Super Bowl Championship game.

I don't think this is a disaster for Malcolm Glazer. It would have been nice to start his reign with a pennant, but it's not that bad that we took the loss. After all, he's only been in charge for a week!

He definitely needs some help from the Manchester players though. Nistelrooy's red-zone offense was awful in this game. He looked like he couldn't finish a bottle of Sunny D. Although to be fair, your teeth do start hurting after a while.

May 24 — Manchester: the future

So, after losing the SA Super Bowl Championship final, my beloved Manchester franchise won zilch this regular season.

Luckily, I have full confidence that Super Malcolm can sort this out.

Here's what he needs to do:

The D is okay, but there is one player that could make it better – Alexei Lalas. He rocks! The club store could sell Lalas-beards, bringing in more money to the franchise's under-developed merchandizing store.

Secondly, Manchester clearly don't kick enough scores. So I understand the Glaz-meister is going to trade for Tampa Bay Buccaneers kicker Matt Bryant to be the new offenser. His longest score last season was from 54 yards, which is 52 yards further than Rude Nistelrooy.

Nistelrooy, meanwhile, can be sent to the Buccaneers in return. I think he proved that he could be an NFL kicker in the SA Bowl. He certainly seemed good at getting the ball over the bar.

May 25 — What are Manchester fans protesting at?

I read that lots of Manchester fans are protesting against 'the bearded multimillionaire American who is out to spoil everyone's fun'. But I really don't understand what they are protesting at. George Lucas isn't that bad! Revenge of the Sith is pretty good!

On top of complaining that C3PO is too camp, people are also saying that the Glaz-meister's takeover of Manchester is a bad thing. How is that possible?

He's taken over a team that hasn't won a pennant for years and is aiming to take them to heights they have never previously experienced. It's not like Manchester could get any lower.

Everyone is comparing my beloved Manchester with the Leeds Enrons. Pop says they had great success, but then ran out of money and had to pawn all their best kickers. Alan Smith and Ferdinand Rio both came to Manchester, while Robbie Fowler is still stuck in a pawnshop in West Yorkshire.

But it's not an entirely bad thing to be compared with them – they got through to the semi-finals of the Euro Series. I'd love Manchester to be able to do that someday!

May 26 – Can Manchester be as big as Liverpool?

The Liverpool Reds are the new Euro Series pennant winners after a come-from-behind victory over Milan AC, who come from Italy (is that really in Europe?).

Again it went to a 12-yard kick-ball challenge but three Milan players did a Scholes – which means missing and then bursting into tears.

It was an incredible game before that as Milan AC sped into a three-to-zip advantage over the Reds, thanks to two scores from Herman Crespo, an offenser who struggled in the EPL last year due to what the air in Britain did to his perm.

But the Liverpool Reds fought their way back into the game in the second period, getting three scores in just six incredible minutes. I desperately hope I live to see the day when Manchester could hit two scores in a couple of minutes in a Euro Series final, let alone three. I don't suppose it would ever happen.

It's the fifth time the Reds have been the best team in Europe. Manchester has won the European Series twice, but one was way back in the 1960s before soccer really existed, so it doesn't really count.

Because the Liverpool Reds come from the north of England, there is a big hatred between them and Manchester, who of course come from the south.

But it's time for Manchester to admit . . . the Liverpool Reds are a big, successful roster and Manchester are not. The sooner Glazer comes in and sorts us out the better. Then maybe we can at least be one of the best eight teams in Europe!

May 27 — EPL rulebook

I've been a Manchester fan for a while now – and no one can say I'm a glory hunter, as we've not won any pennants at all in that time. But after all this time rooting for Manchester, I feel I know enough about soccer to tell you the key rules.

1) The main idea is to kick a score past the other team's goaltender. You can do this by a head-kick or by a kick-kick.

2) Having followed the SA Super Bowl and the Euro Series final, I understand every game is split into four periods – two of 45 minutes and two of 15. Then there is a 12-yard kick-ball challenge and the team who kicked the most scores at the end of all of that gets the win.

3) As the end of the game approaches, the referee speaks to Sir Fergie, who tells him how much time to add on for injuries.

4) Offside in soccer is the same as offside in football – when a player moves too quickly at kick-off. Apparently, it's to stop score-zone hanging, but I've never seen a player hanging off the horizontal bar like a monkey. Pop says that the last person he saw acting like a monkey on the field is former Manchester player Peter Reid.

5) There is a strict etiquette in the game. The following are the worst things you can do on a soccer field, in order of horribleness:
   – Spit at someone
   – Not throw the ball back to the opponent when they kick it out due to an injury
   – Punch someone
   – Kick an opponent knee-high
   – Kick an opponent ankle-high
   – Be Robbie Savage.
   The following are things that it is perfectly fine for

you to do on a soccer field:
- Swear like a trucker
- After being brushed by an opponent, roll around on
  the floor as if you are trying to put out a small fire
  on your jersey.

6) A head coach cannot criticize a referee in any way. A
   kicker, however, is allowed to chase the referee about
   50 yards and tell him exactly what he thinks about
   his mother. Yet if a kicker says a single word to the
   line judge, he is automatically shown a yellow piece
   of paper (yellow is meant to be a soothing color I
   think).

7) Punching is not allowed, unless you are the
   goaltender. Because of this, the people that tend goals
   are anti-social elements who just like punching people
   – see Peter Schmeichel for an example. Another piece
   of proof – Pop says that Sylvester Stallone used to be
   a goaltender, playing for the country of his birth –
   Alliesland – against Germany. And they won, thanks
   to Rocky's last-minute 12-yard kick-ball block. What
   an escape and what a victory that was. First, a great
   soccer man and then an actor. Is there anything
   Stallone can't do? Apart from act, obviously.

8) Fisting is not allowed, unless you are the goaltender.

9) Tripping is not allowed, unless you are Adrian Mutu.

10) Kickers are no longer allowed to take their jerseys off
    to celebrate getting a score. This was a rule brought in
    to make lady soccerers such as Carla Cudicini feel
    more comfortable.

May 28 – Manchester can learn from Britain

As I mentioned earlier, the Britain soccer roster are in the
US of A at the moment, as they get ready to play Team USA
in a nation-on-nation super-clash exhibition at the Bruce
Arena in Chicago.
  I was really looking forward to seeing some of my

Manchester players in action, but due to our non-winning season, GB coach Sven Eriksson has left out all my heroes! Wayne Roonaldo, Ferdinand Rio, Gary Neville and Roy Keano are all seen as not good enough for Britain.

I think this shows just how much Manchester need to get better next series. This Sven guy thinks that Peter Crouch is better than Wayne Roonaldo and he's the Britain coach, so I imagine he is the best British head coach there is. Maybe Sir Fergie should trade Roonaldo for Crouch.

Crouch plays for South Hamptons, who don't even have a Major League side. He is originally from Scotland and used to take part in the Highland games, until the unfortunate time when someone mistook him for a caber and tossed him 30 yards.

Meanwhile, this Keiron Richardson dude in the Britain side looks awesome for a rookie. Maybe Manchester should sign him too.

May 29 – Manchester to trade Shaun 'Right' Phillips?

I read on the internet that Euro Series holders Liverpool Reds are trying to trade for Shaun 'Right' Phillips of Manchester. I never even knew he played for us!

What is Sir Fergie doing? He picks players like Roy Keano and Darren Fletcher who can't get on the Britain roster, yet he ignores a Britain player like Phillips. He's never even been given a spot in the starting rotation for Manchester!

Phillips is the son of former London Arsenals offenser Ian Wright, but changed his name by deed poll in embarrassment after his Dad's woeful Saturday-night 'entertainment' show – The National Lottery Wright Around the World.

By the way, Phillips's nickname is 'Right', because he could never remember which side he was meant to play on, so the other kickers tattooed the word 'Right' on the back of his hand.

I made an error in my last post when I said Manchester

should draft Keiron Richardson. Pop tells me he actually used to be a Manchester player! He was with us six months ago, before Sir Fergie traded him to the Western Bromwiches. He turned the Bromwiches from a bottom side to a fourth bottom side – enough to ensure that they would be playing EPL soccer again next series.

Yet he was awesome in the Bruce Arena, kicking two scores – the first an amazing 23-yard free shot scenario – as Britain beat Team USA two to one.

I hope Sir Fergie changes his mind and brings him back to the Nike Trafford Ballpark.

May 30 – Manchester MUST draft super Diego

We don't get much news about Spanish soccer over here, but I heard that a guy called Diego Forlan from Real Villa, the sister team of the Aston Holiday Homes, hit the most scores in Europe this season.

This means he won the Golden Shoe. Imagine how good he would be if he played in boots rather than shoes! And seeing as the Spanish divisional games are more difficult than the EPL, he must be good.

Forlan comes from Uruguay and is named after soccer legend Diego Maradona, who is famous for using his hand, taking drugs and being fat. So a lot like Robert Downey Jr.

Why doesn't Sir Fergie trade for him? I think he'd be a big success at Manchester. I can't see how a kicker that good could fail to get scores for a team like us!

June 1 – Brazil star Rio in trouble

Manchester's Brazilian star Ferdinand Rio is in a bit of trouble at the moment.

The defenseman was questioned by police in the Swedish town of Ikea after he got into a brawl while at the bachelorette party of his girlfriend Jody Morris.

Rio allegedly urged Jody to stamp on a reporter's head,

which seems silly as the reporter would be able to see up her skirt.

Sir Fergie was furious when he read about this, especially as Rio has yet to agree a new deal with Manchester and is considering testing the free agent market.

The head coach has threatened to kick Rio out of Manchester if he doesn't sign soon, but I'm sure Rio is just being forgetful. It certainly wouldn't be the worst thing he forgot to do.

June 2 — Manchester are the champions! We rock!

I take everything I said back! Manchester did not have a non-winning series this year. I just found out that we won the Barclays SA Premier Reserve League Shield play-off final against the Charlton Addicts practise squad.

Go Buccs!

Why is an unsuccessful head coach like Sir Fergie still in charge of Manchester when we could have Sir Michael Phelan instead? He is definitely the man to get our winningest players into the starting roster. Here's my guide to some of the stars of the next series for Manchester.

Sylvan Ebanks-Blake

An offenser with a typically indigenous name from his home of Cambridge. He is a bustling kicker with an eye for the score-zone and a leg that snaps on a fairly regular basis. File him next to Ole Solskjaer.

Phil Bardsley

A cornerback who made his rookie appearance in a defeat to the Western Bromwiches. Sir Fergie was so angry, he sent him to Belgium, which is worse than any punishment I can think of. He's now back and hoping to edge out Jono Shea from the starting roster.

Paul McShane

Signed from the Maplins Holiday Camp in Wales after he fell out with head coach Ruth Madoc. He's a bit chubby for a soccerer, but he makes up for his lack of mobility with a fine quiff.

Gerard Pique

A defenseman from Catatonia who we drafted from the Barca Loners, a franchise full of social inadequates. He still has some problems fitting into society and prefers not to talk to people like Gary Neville and Darren Fletcher, but then wouldn't we all.

June 5 — Making Manchester a big franchise

My Pop has been telling me how Super Malcolm is going to try to make Manchester a big franchise.

He says that there is lots of money to be made from the Asian market and it would be a good move to trade for some soccermen from there. There are rumors that we are keen to draft Asian star Park Ji-Sung from PSG Eindhoven, the same franchise we drafted Rude Nistelrooy, Jaap Stam and Gabriel Heinze from.

Apparently, we had some Asian players ages ago. Eric Canton was Chinese, while Mark Bosnich came from Australia. I think Sun Jihai is part of Manchester's minor league roster.

All our biggest rivals have already tapped this market. The London Arsenals have Freddy Liung Berg from Singapore, while the Liverpool Reds have half-Korean half-Portugalese star Jose Mi.

Pop also says that my fellow Manchester supporters pay lots to have the names of their favorite kickers on the back of their jerseys. He says that's where EPL franchises make the most money.

So I've been doing some research and maybe Sir Fergie

should trade for a Hollandish man called Jan Vennegoor of Hesselink. The name would cost loads. Glazer can even charge extra for the spaces!

The Aston Holiday Homes also have a player I would like to see at Manchester – Eric Djemba-Djemba. What a great idea! The genius Glazer could decide to write everyone's name twice! I would love a uniform with Rude Nistelrooy-Nistelrooy on the rear.

June 6 – Manchester trade for new goaltender

Sir Fergie has made his first trade of the summer. The Manchester head coach has signed Hollandish goaltender Eddie Vandersar from the Fulham Fayeds.

Eddie is a fine goaltender, conceding only 60 scores in 38 games last series, although how can he be as good as American marvel-legend Timmy Howard?

My biggest worry for the trade is that Eddie didn't hit a single score last series. In fact, he never hit a score the whole time he played in the EPL.

I thought Sir Fergie was trying to increase our score ratio. This isn't going to help!

Still, I'm sure he'll get on great with the Manchester players.

June 8 – Manchester sign three Glazers

Three of Malcolm Glazer's sons have moved to Manchester soccer roster. Joel, Avram and Bryan will all be non-kicking members of the roster. So a bit like Eddie Vandersar, I think.

They replace a man called Roy Gardener, who played in the position of chairman. I'm not sure yet what position the Glazer triplets will play.

I read that the first thing the brothers will do is tell Sir Fergie that he will be out if he doesn't win the EPL Championship game for Manchester this series. This is a win-win situation for us – we either get the pennant or we get rid of the man stopping us winning the pennant.

I'd be happier than my Pop in McDonald's if we won, but the reality is that we won't. We have to somehow compete with the big three in Britain – the London Chelseas, London Arsenals and Liverpool Reds. We don't really have a chance of winning, so Sir Fergie will go and Sir Phelan can get the head coach role!

June 9 – The Glaz-meister to get rid of Sir Charlton

Sir Bob Charlton is going to be cut from the Manchester roster by Super Malcolm Glazer.

The former Ireland Shamrocks head coach has been a non-playing member on the roster since he made a few appearances for Manchester back in the 1930s when soccer was known as 'football'.

Pop says Sir Charlton used to be famous for a comb-over, which is a soccer skill similar to the step-over.

I think it's a good move to get rid of him. After all, wouldn't it have been a conflict of interests, seeing his family already own another EPL side – the Charlton Addicts?

Apparently Sir Charlton gets on really well with Sir Ferguson. Perhaps it's because they have the same first name.

June 10 – Glazer to make Manchester awesome!

Malcolm Glazer has finally broken his silence and told everyone how he is going to make the Manchester franchise the biggest in soccer.

PR expert Glazer leaked a document to the London *Times* which revealed that he can increase profits at Manchester by a huge 50%, simply by putting ticket prices up and restricting money spent on the team. Is he a genius or what!

The Glaz-meister says that he has given Sir Ferguson a massive 25 million English dollars to spend on new trades *every* season. That's awesome! Considering we inked deals for David Beckham and Ryan Giggs for nothing, imagine how good we are going to become with that many bucks!

The news that ticket prices at the Nike Trafford Ballpark will go up is also good news. Not only is it a great money-making scheme, but it also means I might be able to get a seat in the bleachers when I come over to London.

June 13 — Manchester fans back Glazer!

Manchester fans have backed Super Malcolm Glazer's takeover.

My soccer franchise reported they had sold a record number of bleacher series tickets at the Nike Trafford Ballpark for the new series! That's awesome!

Some people had said Manchester fans that don't like the Glaz-meister (how can you not like the Glaz-meister?) would refuse to give any money to the franchise, because he is trying to destroy it.

They said they would burn their series tickets, which seems to me both a huge waste of money and an even bigger drain on the world's paper. The very least they could do would be to recycle their tickets, or wipe their butts on them. It's our children's planet!

Now I may only be 12, but it seems to me that the people refusing to spend any money at the franchise are the people that are going to destroy it.

Get behind the franchise! It's the only way we'll become a big soccer roster and be able to compete with our local rivals the Chelseas and the Arsenals.

June 15 — Christmas cancelled

Old Manchester goaltender Roy Carroll has been drafted by the Western Hammers.

The glovesman, who is nicknamed Christmas because good performances only come around once a year, has moved to the EPL expansion franchise on a no-dollar relocation deal.

His most famous moment in a Manchester uniform was a magic trick against Tott Nam last series, when he threw the ball into his own score-zone, but then with a sleight of hand, pulled it back out without anyone noticing.

He's not that good a magician though – 68,000 people worked out how he did the trick. Only two didn't, but they were the referee and the line judge.

June 19 — What are the mad Manchester fans doing?

Manchester fans are trying to get us kicked out of the Euro Series! What the heck are they doing? (Sorry for the bad language, Pop.) Are they mad?

All of the Manchester supporters angry with Super Malcolm Glazer owning the franchise stormed into a meeting of UESA, who own the Euro Series division. As many as 20 fans showed up to the protest, so watch out for the masses, Malcolm!

They argued that any franchise in this much debt should not be allowed to play in the Euro Series. It's not Glazer's fault the franchise is in so much debt! He's trying to get them out of their money problems!

Surely we want to win the Euro Series final to prove we are as good as the Liverpool Reds. I know we have a long way to go to prove that we can win the tournament, but that is no reason not to bother at least trying.

Meanwhile, Manchester has lost out to the London Chelseas for the third time this series. The first two were dominant losses on the gridiron, but this time, the game is over a man called Jon Obiwan Mikel, who is from the African town of Nigeria.

He agreed to join Manchester, but had a look around and decided he didn't want to join us and now wanted the Chelseas to draft him instead. I guess this is the moment when Obiwan joins the Dark Side. Still, I hear he is a pretty good soccer player for a middle-aged beardy dude.

But, how are we going to become as big a franchise as they are if our own fans try to stop us playing in the best Bowl game in the world?

June 21 — Ole Ole, Ole Ole

Wonderkid Ole Solskjaer could rejoin the Manchester roster for the new series.

The Scandinavia national franchise kicker has spent the past two years on the Injured Reserve list after having surgery on his ACL.

However, 12-year-old Solskjaer, nicknamed Gunner because he is constantly telling his team-mates what he's Gunner be when he grows up, is now fit and ready to help Manchester break the dominance of the London Chelseas.

I'm very excited by this. Pop says Solskjaer kicked one of the scores when we last won the Euro Series final, sometime in the last century. I think I'm right in saying Solskjaer is still the only foetus to score in a Euro Series final.

So he must be better that Rude Nistelrooy and Wayne Roonaldo, who couldn't even get us into the last eight of the European Division last series.

June 23 — 'Stanley' Park moves to Manchester

Manchester has traded for their second man of the summer.

Park Ji-Sung has finally arrived from Manchester's 'feeding club' PSG Eindhoven after the London Chelseas had threatened to come in with a bigger trade to stop us having him.

The Asia star, nicknamed Stanley due to his love of American slapstick movies, was MVP in PSG's run to the semi-Championship game in the Euro Series this year, where his franchise narrowly lost out to Milan AC.

Pop tells me that Manchester have brought Park in to sell more shirts. I think it's a good idea to get a manager for the Manchester merchandizing Megastore, but I think I'd prefer the 4 million English dollars to be spent on new soccer stars.

Park kicked 13 scores for PSG after they drafted him from Korean side the Kyoto Purple Swords three years ago. However, he did increase jersey sales by 3.4%, which is impressive. However, I am under the impression he has little DVD sales experience and he is not completely familiar with the replica shrimp sandwiches that are on sale at the Nike Trafford Ballpark.

June 24 — The legends of Manchester

Manchester has a pretty good team now, but Pop tells me that in the distant past, we had the best team in the British league.

So I sat down with Pop and made him tell me all about the best kickers in Manchester's long 13-year history.

David Beckham

The best kicker Manchester has ever had, Beckham once kicked a score from the other side of the 50-yard line! Beckham is one of the most famous men on the planet, along with singer George Michael. They both have a lot in common. For one, they like to spend their free time hanging around Loos.

Eric Canton

A martial arts expert from China, Canton is remembered more for his Kung Fu than for his skills. Traded from the

Leeds Enrons, his soccer ball control was almost as good as his zen mind control.

Peter Schmeichel

Schmeichel was a brilliant goaltender, who had a 93% throwing ratio on passes over 50 yards! Was a favorite of Sir Ferguson's as they had regular competitions over who had the reddest nose.

Teddy Sheringham

Sheringham hit one of the scores as Manchester won the Euro Series final against Bayern Munchers. Pop tells me he had a yard of pace in his head, which is the only pace he ever had. Amazingly, he is still kicking in the EPL for the Western Hammers, despite now needing the help of a zimmer frame to move about.

Mark Hughes

Pop says Mark Hughes was a great offenser. His most famous score came in a Euro Series game when he scored with a spectacular BMX-kick from the 18-yard line. He's now the head coach of the Blackburn Pyros, a northern prison team about 200 miles north of the Nike Trafford Ballpark.

Carol Poborsky

The only woman every to play for Manchester, but you'd have thought she'd have toned down her wild hair to fit into the man's world of soccer. Not very good, but she did always have the cleanest kit on the roster.

Jordi Cruyff

Even I have heard the name Cruyff – one of the most famous names in soccer. The man is a legend and I can't believe he played for Manchester. He is best known for inventing a new turn, which in Jordi's case was turning from his position and trotting to the sideline when the line judge held up his number.

Michael Phelan

Not a legend on the field, but a legend off it. Sir Phelan was the winningest head coach at Manchester last series and it is only a matter of time before he replaces Sir Ferguson.

June 27 — Who Manchester should trade for

Manchester's kickers started summer camp today as they prepare for the new series and it's time for Sir Fergie to hurry up and finalize his depth chart.

So far we have traded for Park Ji-Sung from the country of Asia and Hollandish international Eddie Vandersar. But we finished seven games behind the London Chelseas last series, so there is a lot of work to be done. Here is the list of the kickers I think we should draft:

Theodore Zagorakis

Zagorakis was named MVP in the Eurovision Soccer Contest last year. Pop says he did very well for the Leicester Crisp Packets (we'd call them the Chip Packs) when he was with them and could be a great addition to our central line-up.

Robert Fowler

Fowler, the son of Arthur and Pauline, had a magnificent scoring record for the Liverpool Reds during his time there, but Manchester drafted him two seasons ago and he hasn't played once. What is Sir Fergie thinking of? If he was good enough for the Euro Series champions, then he must be good enough for us. Time to call him up from Manchester's minor league roster.

Ronald Inyo

I've been doing some research and I've found out that Ronald Inyo is the best kicker in the world. He currently plays for the Barca Loners, a group of anti-social individuals who pick up great skills at a young age because no one talks to them and a football is their only friend. I know he is at a better franchise at the moment, but from the Loners, even Rude Nistelrooy will seem like a nice guy! And that's saying something.

Diego Forlan

As I mentioned earlier, he is exactly what Manchester need. He hit more scores last season than anyone else in Europe, so I can't see any way that he could be a failure in Manchester.

With these players, along with the ones we have already, I think we will improve our percentage to over .600 which should be enough to get us into second in the EPL – higher than we've been for a long time!

June 28 — The London Chelseas Power Show

Although Manchester has improved, the EPL champions London Chelseas have been trading more than us.

First up, they drafted Frank Arnesen for 10 million English dollars from Tott Nam, a team that specialize in young Vietnamese players. Now, I know Chelsea have a lot of bucks since being taken over by Russia, but surely this is too expensive even for them.

I mean, Arnesen is OK, but he's in his 50s and his pace has gone completely. He won't kick many scores and I can't see him helping out the defensemen at all. Pop says: 'He's going to be a bigger dud than Drogba and Kez, man!'

However, the London Chelseas' head coach Roman Abramovich is still looking for other offensers. They have drafted Herman Crespo from Milan AC, the player who kicked two scores in the Euro Series final and will be a big hit in the EPL.

They are also expected to trade for our very own Shaun Phillips. It's bad enough that Sir Fergie doesn't rate him and refuses to put him in the starting roster. But to then trade him to the EPL champion franchise – well that's just too much.

Asier Del Horno has also come in and is now officially the most expensive kicker to have a name that meant he was bullied mercilessly at junior high.

Meanwhile, Ji-Sung Veron has been traded to International Milan. The Argentinia player used to play for Manchester, but he was lured away by the thought of playing for a bigger franchise and moved to the Chelseas.

June 29 – Glazers meet the Soccer Association

The Glazer family have had their first meeting with the Soccer Association.

Super Malcolm now owns 98% of Manchester soccer franchise, but I'm very confident he'll get the remaining 3% very soon.

The Glaz-meister's three sons met SA chief David Davies, who Pop says has a reputation as 'a bit of a player', but I can't find any record of him in soccer!

Also in the meeting was Tony Blair's soccer senator Richard Caborn as Joel, Bryan and Avi convinced them what all Manchester fans know – that they will make us great again.

Joel Glazer said the family had 'a passion to keep Manchester successful' which is slightly worrying. Why would he want to maintain the level of success? Do we want to finish third in the standings every year? Surely we want to get better!

June 30 — Manchester fans show support for Glazers

Manchester fans turned up to give their support to the Glazers yesterday evening.

The Glazer triplets visited the Nike Trafford Ballpark for the first time following their meeting with the SA and over 300 fans turned up to greet them.

My fellow Manchester fans chanted 'Die Glazers Die', a touching German song which Pop says means 'The Glazers The'. What a wonderful way to show their support! No one who speaks German could ever be a danger to anyone else.

Some of them had jerseys on saying 'Shareholders United'. What they actually meant was 'Shareholder United' – Super Malcolm Glazer is the only shareholder of the franchise now.

 ## July 1 — Glazers lay out plans for Manchester

Malcolm Glazer's three sons have laid out their plans for the future of the Manchester franchise.

Big Joel, wearing the Manchester jersey that is famous across the British Home Counties, said: 'This franchise has such a rich history and tradition, so we are not looking to change that or touch that.'

He's right. This franchise has been around for over 13 years now and the Glazers were never going to storm in here and destroy all that history. Surely you Brits can trust us Americans with a bit of history!

The Glazer triplets also said that Manchester would definitely be after a player like Wayne Roonaldo if he becomes available. That's awesome! We already have two Roonaldos . . . does anyone know how many more brothers there are?

It was nice to see the fans showing up to welcome the Glaz-meister's sons to the Nike Trafford Ballpark. Many of them tried to put barriers up to stop them leaving. Look how they've taken the Glazers into their hearts! They don't want them to leave!

Some of them also threw coins at them, which is nice because everyone knows they have borrowed money to buy Manchester. The fans are trying to help them pay it back!

There are a couple of Manchester fans who were worried when, asked about money, Jolly Joel said that there was not a bottomless pit. Well, I think they are wrong. I heard that there was a bottomless pit and that Liam Miller was believed to have fallen into it.

July 3 — Ask Roswell

All the news about Manchester at the moment is how the fans are taking the Glazer triplets to their hearts. So I thought it was time to answer a batch of your e-mails. These are genuine e-mails that readers of the Manchester Buccaneers website sent in.

STEVE from UK: As a lifelong Liverpool Reds fan, I'd love to know what you think of our team's chances in the Euro Series first round against a great team from the city of Wales, the Total Network Solutions.

ROSWELL: I'm confused, Steve. How are the Total Network Solutions even in the Euro Series this year? I've had a look and they are not even in the EPL! It says they are champions of Wales, but why do they have their own pennant? Next Wales will want to have a national roster of their own as well! Pop went over to Britain last year and he said he couldn't find the city of Total Network Solutions at all. He wanted to go because he heard they do lots of dancing on the streets there.

ASHWIN from London: Yo dude, just e-mailing u 2 know . . . on ur recent blog – The London Chelseas Power Show – in msn spaces u mentioned tht chelsea r tryin 2 draft crespo 4m ACmilan but dude he's already a Chelseas player who has just been loaned out to

ACmilan . . . get ur stats right kid . . . & wht's this shit about Arnesen . . . dude do u know who he is . . . he is not a player dude . . . he is the best god damn scout . . . who identifies young knights . . .

P.S. – All Man U . . . fans seem to be dudes man!!!

ROSWELL: I'm sorry Ashwin, I'm doing my best. My passion is for the Manchester franchise, not the London Chelseas one. I've got a question for you though . . . if Arnesen identifies young knights, are the Chelseas entering some kind of jousting league this year?

IDIOTEQUE 24 from Manchester: YOU STUPIDD RETARD, R U A SPASTIC OR SUMIN?? DO YOU HAVE ANNNY IDEA WHAT YOU GOING ON ABOUT? THIS IS FOOTBALL U STUPID IDIOT, GO AND PLAY WIV UR BABRY DOLS OR SOMETVING COz you aint got no place in footbal alRIGHT U LITTLE YANK AND UU CAN TAK THAT FAT GINGER GLAZIER WIV U MAN UTD IS NOT FOR SALE, NEVA HAS BEN, NEVA WILL BEe.

THIS IS PROBS THE WORSTT SITE I've eva seen most of ur stuff is unelastic AND ITSS ROY KEANE U DUMB Azzz not keanoo (AND HE IS aABOUT 10 TIMES BETTER THAN GERRARD GETT UR STATZ RIGHT BEFORE U CUM UP WITH THAT)

im righting complainn ur intternet providr to get you sud coz u cant put rong informationz on the internet itz ilegal u dumbazz U BETTERR TAKKE DIS SITE OF OR U GONA HAVE IN TROUBLE.

ROSWELL: I'm sorry Idioteque. I don't speak British.

July 5 – Manchester must sign Stevie Wonder

Oh my God! Liverpool Reds superstar Stevie Gerrard has asked to be traded from the Euro Series holders.

Gerrard, who double-footedly dragged the Reds back from three-zip down against Milan AC, has decided not to ink a contract extension at Ann's Field.

I used to think that he only used to be in the starting rotation because he was the son of head coach Houllier

Gerrard, but he has really improved year-on-year.

He is now expected to join the London Chelseas in a trade for over 75 million English dollars! That's about the amount raised by Live8 in Philadelphia! Still, let's hope the money it brings in can help make poverty history in Liverpool.

I think Manchester should definitely try to draft him. This guy is awesome. He's just like Roy Keano. Except he can still run! He can tackle, usually with both feet at the same time. He can kick scores. He is one of the best British players around.

By the way, if you're wondering, Gerrard is nicknamed Stevie Wonder. I think this is because he is sometimes blind to the option of passing to team-mates instead of shooting from the 30-yard line.

July 6 — Olympic-sized U-turn from Stevie

What an incredible day! First London somehow beat New York to host the 2012 Olympics. Being a Manchester fan, I love London as much as anyone, but better than New York? Are you mad?

London is smelly and full of crime and pigeons, with a transport system so old that Eddie Vandersar can remember it opening. How can that compare with New York? The Big Apple doesn't have many pigeons.

But after all that, an even more amazing thing happened. Stevie Gerrard, with his pen just about to start signing his name on the London Chelseas contract, performed a U-turn and decided to stay with the Liverpool Reds.

Having said he wanted to be traded, he now says it was all a big misunderstanding and he's going nowhere. He'll probably decide to leave again tomorrow, but it's bad for us at the moment.

If he was on the 2012 Olympic committee, he'd announce tomorrow that London only got the games due to lots of confusion and that he meant to say that New York will host them after all. Is U-turning on Olympic sport?

Despite this setback for the London Chelseas, Manchester seem to be getting left behind in the battle to challenge for the EPL pennant this series.

I read that the Liverpool Reds are set to draft Peter Crouch, one of my favorite players, for a bargain 15 million English dollars from the South Hamptoms.

Crouch, who played college hoops before turning to soccer, is of course ahead of Wayne Roonaldo in Sven Eriksson's World Cup team having played in the tour of the USA in May. He's probably the best head-kicker in the EPL.

Meanwhile, the London Arsenals, who were the scoringest team in the British soccer league last series, are trying to trade for a Brazilian striker, Rob Inyo, brother of Ronald. And the London Chelseas, already 18 games ahead of us in last season's championship, are set to steal Shaun 'Right' Phillips from Manchester's minor league side.

All we've done is draft a Korean man to sell shirts in the Megastore and a veteran goaltender who has never hit a single score! We might be out of contention before the all-star break!

July 10 — A song for Glazer

One of the tiny minority of Manchester fans who hasn't fallen under the Glaz-meister's spell has written a song against Super Malcolm.

It's being done by Peter Hook, who used to be in the rock combo New Order. They were famous for the soccer anthem 'World in Motion', which was adopted by the Britain roster for World Cup XIV in 1990. Paul Gazza hated it so much that he couldn't stop crying.

Anyway, Hook is releasing a new CD about how Glazer is bad for soccer, but I think it's garbage. I think I could do a much better job, so I've had a go.

By the way, it was going to have a chorus that went 'Go Buccs', but I couldn't think of anything that rhymes with Buccs.

'A Song for Glazer'

A man from the States started watching some soccer,
He already had an NFL team in his locker,
So he looked at the standings to see who was best,
But the Chelseas weren't cheap, so he looked at the rest.
Manchester were a team that he'd seen on a vid,
So he combed his red beard and he put in a bid.

(Chorus)
Glazer! Glazer!
He's our savior! Savior!
So let's pull our pants right up to our chest,
The Glaz-meister's going to make Manchester best.

The Manchester fans were seething with rage,
But Glazer relaxed like an intelligent sage,
He looked at their comments and started to yawn,
As idiots said he looked like a leprechaun,
They threatened him with violence and one mentioned
  cyanide,
But Malc stayed in Tampa and decided to try an' hide.

(Chorus)
Glazer! Glazer!
He's our savior! Savior!
So let's pull our pants right up to our chest,
The Glaz-meister's going to make Manchester best.

So if you want a franchise that will win some Bowls,
If you want for lunch some delightful prawn rolls,
If you want a franchise whose stadium roars,
If you want a roster who will kick lots of scores,
If you want a Megastore bigger than Sears,
The team to support's the Manchester Buccaneers.

(Chorus)
Glazer! Glazer!
He's our savior! Savior!
So let's pull our pants right up to our chest,
The Glaz-meister's going to make Manchester best.

July 12 – Spector becomes an Addict

American speedy whizzkid Johnny Spector has been forced to join the Charlton Addicts for a year.

The left cornerback is moving into the residential Outreach program in an attempt to cure his obsession with Kerplunk. I know it is addictive, but it is terrible to miss a whole soccer series because of it.

The left cornerback is seen as a potential national franchise kicker and it is another mega-mistake by Sir Fergie letting him get into this situation. Oooh! This is going to make the Glaz-meister mad. Not only are we losing a great young kicker, but a great young American kicker.

What's even worse is that the Addicts haven't given us a single English dollar for him! It just leaves Timmy Howard as the only American on the roster and he probably won't play after Eddie Vandersar was drafted in.

Spector has a revolutionary way of playing. He makes a Wall of Sound in an attempt to put off the other team's offensers. I'm not sure how it works, but it sounds amazing.

July 13 – Sir Fergie says: It's good to talk

Sir Ferguson has revealed his reasons for drafting goaltender Eddie Vandersar and they are the stuff of a rambling idiot.

The Manchester head coach said he went for the Hollandish goaltender because he speaks English.

Well Sir Fergie, if you wanted someone who speaks English, why not sign an American goaltender? And what's wrong with Timmy Howard anyway? He can speak almost perfect English, even if he does accidentally add in a swear word.

Anyway, I just don't understand how having a goaltender that can talk is going to be useful. Wayne Roonaldo only knows words with four letters in them, while central defensemen Ferdinand Rio and Michael Silvester aren't English anyway.

How about trading for someone who is good at kicking scores, not someone whose main ability is to be able to talk?

July 14 — Ireland star leaves the London Arsenals

The London Arsenals are expected to lose their offensive captain today as Italian side the Uventus Barcodes are set to draft Paddy Vieira.

Irish star Vieira, along with his countryman Gilbert O'Silva, have been the heart and soul of the Arsenals' middle for a number of years, both helping them to a perfect series last year.

But his departure is a huge boost to Manchester as we aim to move up to the runners-up spot in the EPL. I'm sure fans of the London Arsenals will miss the shout around the Hi Berry Stadium for Vieira: 'He comes from Donegal, He plays for the Arsenals.'

With Vieira gone and Edu returning to Brazil to pick up the rest of his name, the London Arsenals are very short of middlemen for the upcoming series.

Other than Gilbert O'Silva, they only have 16-year-old Matthew Flamini and 13-year-old Chesc Fabregas to play in the central middleman positions. Maybe we can trade Liam Miller to them. If we can remember which one he is again.

Meanwhile, the Liverpool Reds are looking stronger than ever. Already officially the best team in Europe after winning the Euro Series, the Reds hammered Total Network Solutions three-zip. And TNS have a championship-winning side, so the Reds must be pretty awesome this series.

July 15 — Pre-series starts tomorrow!

Manchester start their pre-series exhibition games tomorrow as they take on the Clyde Andbonnies.

Sir Fergie obviously rates the Andbonnies, who play in the

northern town of Scotland, highly as he is sending all 11 starters to the game, including the Roonaldo brothers.

I'm not sure why he is so worried about them, as they are in a very low league. As I understand it, the EPL is the top league in Britain, and then there are three minor leagues. When you are demoted from the third of those, you play in the Scottish Premier League, and the Clyde Andbonnies play in the league below that.

Plus, I'm not sure why we are going all the way up north to play . . . that's got to be over 500 miles from the Nike Trafford Ballpark in south England.

July 17 — Clyde Andbonnies 1—5 Manchester

What a start to the new series! We've only played one game and already Manchester has won its first pennant.

Manchester demolished the Clyde Andbonnies five to one to win the Optical Express Challenge Cup. Who needs the SA Bowl when we have that?

And this against a Clyde Andbonnies roster that finished third in their championship last series – the same spot as Manchester finished. It shows we are definitely improving!

Rude Nistelrooy proved he is back to doing what he does best – winning a 12-yard kick-ball punishment – which the reports I read called 'soft'.

Nistelrooy tucked the punishment into the score-zone and grabbed a second score, after World Cup-winning legend Kleberson and SA Bowl loser Paul Scholes had also kicked scores.

More surprising is that Liam Miller also found the score-zone. He hadn't even found the pitch for the last nine months.

It was a great day for Manchester, with just one piece of bad news. Defenseman Ferdinand Rio was greeted with shouts of 'greedy' by Manchester fans every time he touched the ball.

Rio has apparently demanded 200,000 English dollars every week to play for Manchester for the next few series. It's a lot, but it seems fair to me. After all, Rio does have a few expensive habits.

July 18 – Sir Fergie given final warning

Sir Fergie has been told to curb his wild temper and loose tongue by the Soccer Association.

The Manchester head coach claimed sinister forces were at work after Manchester was denied two 12-yard kick-ball punishments in the EPL game at Newcastle last series.

He even went as far as to hire ghost expert Derek Acorah to establish what dark souls are affecting their decisions and was told: 'According to my sources in the other realm, you did not get any decisions because Alan Smith dived. Now leave me alone, I'm trying to chat up Doris Day.'

Sir Fergie also said that the only way one of his kickers was ever going to get a 12-yard kick-ball punishment is if they were shot. Which sounds like a threat to Liam Miller to me.

He was found guilty of improper conduct, wasting the time of a medium and impersonating a gangster.

July 19 – Manchester draft successful goaltender

Manchester has drafted a rookie goaltender called Ben Foster from the Stoke Potteries.

Pop says the Potteries is famous for its cups, so he has obviously won a lot of soccer games. He must be better than Eddie Vandersar, who never won anything at the Fulham Fayeds.

Where does this leave American demi-God Tim Howard? Howard, nicknamed **** because of his love of gasoline, could be our third-choice goaltender next series. The Glaz-meister isn't going to be happy about that!

July 20 — Peter Borough XI 0—6 Manchester

Rude Nistelrooy received a hat from Sir Ferguson as Manchester moved to two and oh in pre-series with a victory over a team selected by Mr Peter Borough, the man famous for founding the franchise the Middle Borough.

The Hollandish star kicked three scores in the 'testimonial' game for Barry Fry. Pop says you get a testimonial if you play for the same franchise for 10 years. But this Barry Fry dude is in his 60s, so he must have started playing soccer really late in life.

However, it's not as good as it sounds. Sir Fergie played his starting roster in the first period and the game was zip-zip. He got angry with them and made 11 replacements and only then did the team start performing.

Cristiano Roonaldo also grabbed two scores and it looks like Manchester will get a lot of scores this series. If we can do it against a Peter Borough XI, we can do it against anyone.

Ferdinand Rio was jeered by the Manchester fans again, who called him a 'London Chelseas Rent Boy'. What does this mean? Will Chelsea try to rent him, instead of trading him for English dollars?

Meanwhile, the London *Sun* newspaper is reporting that Rio and the Roonaldo brothers are in trouble with Sir Fergie after refusing to get the team coach home from the game at the Clyde Andbonnies. The trio instead decided to rent a car and drive back themselves back from the town of Scotland.

The report says that they were unhappy they were not flying home and that seems fair enough. It's a long way from Scotland to the south of England.

Does Manchester have such serious money worries that they can't afford to fly? Easyjet charge just 59 English dollars to fly from Scotland to London Manchester Airport. I know the Glazmeister has a private jet and could help, but I guess he doesn't want the soccer players urinating on the seats and all the other nasty things 'jocks' do.

July 21 — Manchester head from south to east

Manchester have flown out to Asia as part of their pre-series exhibition program.

The franchise start their road trip with an exhibition game against the Hong Kong King Kongs, which is a whole country, so they must be really good.

We then go on to play the Beijing Hondas (who I think are the old franchise of our former Chinese star Eric Canton), Urawa Red Sushis and Kashima Reindeer.

It's a shame we couldn't have played the Clyde Andbonnies next week. With all the airmiles we are getting, we could have flown home from Scotland for free and there wouldn't have been the rows with Ferdinand Rio and the Roonaldo bros.

Right defenseman Gary Neville says he loves visiting Asia. He said: 'The support is unbelievable. You can have thousands of people just literally camping outside the hotel,' completely misunderstanding the problem of homelessness and overpopulation in the area.

July 22 — Glazer's mini-me to the rescue!

One of the Glazer triplets has flown out to Asia to save the future of the Manchester franchise.

Manchester fans have been jeering defenseman Ferdinand Rio for being greedy. Apparently, this all started when Rio hogged the bathroom for two hours before training, as he was so worried about forgetting to pee again.

But Joel Glazer has jetted out to Japan, where Manchester play champions the Beijing Hondas, to draw up a bathroom rota. I think it will be limited to two minutes per person, or four if they take a copy of *Sports Illustrated* in with them.

The Glaz-meister's mini-me also wanted to speak to Cristiano Roonaldo, who is yet to ink a new deal with the franchise, but he has returned to his home in Liverpool to nurse his ill father.

That's a really nice thing to do. He must be the favorite son, as his younger brother Wayne hasn't bothered to go home. I would definitely head home if Pop got ill, especially if I missed a math class in the process.

July 23 — Hong Kong King Kongs 0—2 Manchester

It's official! Manchester is better than a whole country! We moved to three and oh in pre-series with a win over the Hong Kong King Kongs (or Hong KKKs for short).

The scores came from a one-yard sneak by Italian-American rookie Giuseppe Rossi and a clever french fry from 20 yards by Dong Fangzhuo, who comes from Doncaster in Britain.

The Hong Kong King Kongs are no slouches either . . . they recently destroyed the Mighty Macao Maestros eight scores to one and kicked 26 scores to zip against the giants of Guam in two games!

If we can beat a country that good, beating the London Arsenals will be no problem! A perfect series so far . . . the Glazer revolution is in full flow!

July 24 — Rossi, his belly and potato chips

Sir Fergie has been praising little American offenser Giuseppe Rossi following his score-getting debut on the tour of the world's eastern seaboard.

The Manchester head coach was delighted with the way Rossi bundled the soccer ball over the scoring line with his stomach and says he wants to see more organ-related scores.

Sir Fergie went on to say that Rossi reminds him of former Britain star Gary Lineker. I'm not sure exactly what that means, but I assume he's calling Rossi 'Big Ears' and saying he eats too many potato chips.

Dong Fangzhuo also received acclaim from the head coach, who said he is progressing well, but the problem may come in getting him into Britain. He's only small, so one option may be to smuggle him inside someone's suitcase.

The other alternative is to build some kind of Trojan Horse for him to jump out of. Is Rude Nistelrooy from Troy?

July 25 – Crisis as Keano and Sir Fergie fall out!

Oh no! Something terrible has happened. My favorite player Roy Keano has had a big argument with Sir Fergie.

Keano, the best Manchester player to never play for England, was furious that his kids were not treated well enough in the summer camp in the Algarve, which is on the south coast of England I think.

I'm not entirely sure of what the problem was, but I think he thought the other Manchester players were a bad influence on his kids, especially the Roonaldo brothers.

Cristiano was giving them diving tips in the pool, while Wayne was showing them how to dive bomb to soak the old ladies sunbathing (why Wayne would want the old ladies to have wet t-shirts on I have no idea).

The Neville brothers told on them and then ran off to make sure they were in the front row of Sir Fergie's team-talk. Elsewhere, Liam Miller was playing hide and seek and wasn't found for 27 days.

Because of this, Keano has not gone on the tour of the Far East. I heard that he and Sir Fergie had made up, but only in the same way that George W. Bush has made up with the French president.

It's the worse thing that could have happened. Imagine if Keano gets cut and we have to go into the new series with Darren Fletcher and Quinton Fortune as middlemen. It doesn't bear thinking about.

July 27 – Beijing Escorts 0–3 Manchester

Four and oh! The Glaz-meister is clearly proving inspirational for the Manchester players as they extended their perfect pre-series record.

The Beijing Escorts had narrowly lost 3–2 to Portugalese franchise Realmadrid, but today they were humbled by the mighty Manchester Buccaneers.

Paul Scholes notched two scores, although neither of them was from 12 yards obviously! The first was a head-kick from the two-yard line, while the second was a kick-kick from the same distance.

Park Ji-Sung then proved he is more than just the manager of the Megastore, brought in to sell shirts, as he kicked a third score. I think he was only playing as the game was played in the Workers' Stadium, so all the staff got a run-out. I think Carlos Queiroz played 45 minutes, while Martha the tea-maid replaced offenser Rude Nistelrooy (and probably looked more dangerous).

It's been a great pre-series for us. Beating the Hong Kong King Kongs country team is definitely the highlight so far. They had over 7 million players to choose from – we only had 25 on our roster!

July 28 – Kashima Reindeer 2–1 Manchester

An earthquake hit the Kashima Reindeer stadium in Japan, but I felt the tremors in Florida as Manchester slumped to their first loss in pre-series.

There are reports stating that the earthquake was caused by Sir Ferguson as he jumped up and down in anger after Manchester conceded a score.

The tremors measured 2.0 on the Richter Scale, while the epicenter was 100 miles away. According to my geology books, an earthquake of that size isn't enough to cause a tidal wave or destroy tall buildings. But it is just about strong enough to make someone say 'Did you feel that?'

Anyway, we'd won all our previous pre-series games, but it took just four minutes for the Reindeer, who finished fifth in the JPL last year, to notch a score. American super-sensation Timmy Howard was in goal and I can't believe Masashi Motoyama's shot beat him fairly, so it must have hit the ground just as the earthquake struck, knocking the ball into the opposite corner.

Veteran wideout Ryan Giggs level-scored soon after from the four-yard line after a middle from Cristiano Roonaldo, but we were soon behind again as Motoyama hit another no-bounce one-time score.

I was so confident about the new series before this, but now I'm really worried. If we lose to a team that didn't even qualify for the Euro Series, how are we going to cope against better teams from the EPL like the Aston Holiday Homes?

I must say I'm 'quaking' in my boots!

July 29 — The Van's fury at confused Rio

Now I am really concerned. Manchester's team spirit seems to be melting in the Chinese heat.

Ferdinand Rio and Rude 'The Van' Nistelrooy were involved in a huge confrontation after the earthquake-inducing defeat to the Kashima Reindeer.

As I understand it, Nistelrooy, who has a temper like a white-van driver who has just been cut up by a middle-aged woman driving a Range Rover in the center of town, was furious that Rio has a better recent scoring record than he does and they started screaming at each other as they were walking off the gridiron.

A confused Rio then also aimed a 'V' sign at the Manchester fans, mistakenly thinking that we were actually victorious. Sir Fergie insists he didn't see it.

July 30 — Urawa Red Sushis 0–2 Manchester

It's OK, Manchester fans. We're back on track.

Wayne Roonaldo got his first scores of the pre-series as we moved to five and one, with victory in our final exhibition game in the Asia Tour.

His first was just a faucet-in from five yards, but the second was a piece of David Copperfield-like magic. He waved his magic wand and two defenders disappeared like the Great Wall of China. Then he spotted the goaltender standing on the six-yard line and produced a magnificent french fry into the goal.

Worryingly, neither Ferdinand Rio nor Rude Nistelrooy played, both being left in the naughty corner of the locker room as punishment for their fight in the previous game.

I can understand Rio being aggressive. Coming from Brazil, he's got that Latino temperament. But why is Nistelrooy so hostile? He claims it's from jetlag, but surely being on a long flight just gives you DVT and a stomach-ache from eating a rancid chicken pie.

 August 2 — EPL preview

The new series starts this week with the traditional opening exhibition game, called the Community Shield. Pop says it used to be called something else, but Chelsea wanted the name of the game to reflect their communist roots.

As a preview to the new series, I am going to round up every team's chances, starting with all the pennant-chasers.

THE PENNANT-CHASERS

London Chelseas

The London Chelseas are defending their first EPL pennant and are looking stronger than ever after drafting Shaun 'Right' Phillips from our minor league practice roster.

They have been touring the USA (although they didn't come to Tampa . . . lucky for them!) They played Euro finalists Milan AC and were one and oh, with one tie. They also beat DC United. What kind of a name is DC United? I'm glad Manchester don't have 'United' after their name . . . it sounds horrible!

The Chelseas are favorites to win the EPL again, but they will have to beat the might of Manchester! Don't forget, we still have Phil Neville on our roster! Pop says the USA beat Russia to the moon and I'm hoping we can beat them to the EPL title as well.

Key kicker – Frank Lampard: After appearing on a BBC show called 'Britain's Fattest Soccer Stars', Lampard was forced to go on a diet and it has paid dividends in his career. Now 46 lbs lighter, the middleman has established himself as one of the best in the country. But he still has enough weight behind his kicks to get 30-yard scores.

Worst kicker – Geremi: They drafted him for almost 10 million English dollars to be their reserve Makelelele. He turned out to be more like their reserve Joe Cole and no one wants two Joe Coles in their side.

London Arsenals

The London Arsenals beat us in a 12-yard kick-ball challenge to win the SA Super Bowl in May, but have been weakened by the loss of Irish middleman Paddy Vieira.

Despite this loss – and the lack of Vieira's Irish team-mate Gilbert O'Silva so far in pre-series – they won their first pennant of the new series, beating Ayax and Porto to win the Amsterdam Tournament in Germany. I believe their prize for winning it was an all-you-can-eat trip to the Rossebuurt district of the city.

Amazingly, one of their star kickers, 73-year-old Dennis

 Bergkamp, is afraid of flying and travels to every game by car, even missing some games because of this. I think it's because he grew up travelling everywhere by horse and cart and he's not going to stop just because there's some 'new-fangled technology' out there.

But what a wimp! You'd never get an American hero refusing to get into a plane. I pity the fool that won't fly.

I reckon we can definitely leap over them and finish in the first runners-up spot this series, which would be our highest finish for some time. That would show exactly how much the Glaz-meister has improved Manchester in just one year.

Key kicker – Thierry Henry: Constantly kicks great scores, he is one of the best kickers in the world, although there is no doubt that he is fully aware of that fact. Has extremely bad taste in cars. He is currently trying to learn French and is regularly heard wandering around London saying: 'What is French for Va-Va-Voom?' He keeps calling everybody Bobby as well, which is a bit odd.

Worst kicker – Lauren: The Cameroonian defensewoman is the weak link in the London Arsenals team. I wouldn't want to tell her that though, as I get the feeling she might do to me what she did to Rude Nistelrooy.

Liverpool Reds

The Liverpool Reds were the best team in Europe last series, winning the Euro Series. And they are even better now, having traded for England's top head-kicker Peter Crouch and goaltender Jose Reina. Plus, they have dealt out Antonio Nunez, Igor Biscan and Bruno Cheyrou, which can only make them better.

The franchise from Ann's Field will be a big threat this year. Although, there's something I don't understand. The Liverpool Reds are the best team in Europe, but only ranked fifth in the EPL. They were lucky the Everton Stickies weren't in the Euro Series, as they were better than their neighbours last series.

Key kicker – Peter Crouch: More like Key head-kicker, as there is no better 6 foot 7 soccerer in the EPL. Pop says he's got a good touch for a big man, although that's what they said about Mike Tyson. With a good run on the roster, I reckon he could head-kick at least three scores this series.

Worst kicker – Harry Kewell: Drafted from the Leeds Enrons as one of the most exciting wideouts in the game. And to be fair, he has put in some scintillating performances for the Liverpool Reds minor league team.

Sunderland

Sunderland is a country just north of England, where they speak English, but in a really weird accent that makes it sound like a different language. So a bit like Canada I suppose. They used to have their own division and the national roster won the pennant last series, but they've been allowed to join the EPL this year and will want to top the divisional standings again.

But Manchester shouldn't be scared of meeting a country. We beat Hong Kong in pre-series who are rated 120th in the world, while Sunderland isn't even in the world rankings, so I'm confident we can beat them.

Their best player is Anthony The Tallec, who they are renting from the Liverpool Reds. But I think he is due back via the 24-hour drop-in letterbox at Ann's Field by May 8 at 10pm.

Key kicker – Anthony The Tallec: Anyone from the Liverpool Reds has to be good and he played a key role in their Euro Series victory. He is definitely better than his best friend Florent The Pongolle.

Worst kicker – Kevin Kyle: A poor man's Peter Crouch and you'd have to be very poor to put up with that. He's actually a Scottish nationalist, but I think his Grandma was Sunderlandish.

EURO SERIES HOPEFULS

Tott Nam

During the summer, Tott Nam drafted middlemen Edgar Davids, Wayne Routledge, Aaron Lennon, Tom Huddlestone and Teemu Tainio. I think head coach Martin Jol must be planning a revolutionary new 1–8–1 formation to accommodate all these new kickers.

Davids is a world-class Hollandish national franchise kicker and is famous for wearing sunglasses when he plays. But I think that's just to shade his eyes from the bright yellow pieces of card that he gets shown by referees in every game.

Tott Nam have won the Peace Cup in pre-series, which they will put in their Trophy Room alongside the War Cup – the franchise's last pennant, won during World War II.

Key kicker – Robbie Keano: Roy's brother, who not only

cannot get a game for Britain, but is hardly picked for Tott Nam either. I think he had a good chance of being picked in the British gymnastics team for the Beijing Olympics in 2008. His floor routine, complete with pistol salute, is a definite medal prospect.

Worst kicker – Andy Reid: He likes kicking from the 25-yard line, which is good for a soccer star. But he likes pies more, which is bad for a soccer star. Tott Nam decided to cover an entire building with one of their uniforms, but they didn't need to get a giant one made especially. They just used Andy Reid's jersey.

The Aston Holiday Homes

Pop tells me a way to judge a good kicker is to answer one simple question: has he been traded away by David O'Leary? If he has, then you know he must be good. So I'm looking forward to seeing Darius Vassell, who has just been traded to Manchester from the Holiday Homes. He'll fit in well with Rude Nistelrooy. No doubt Sir Fergie will ignore him and put him on the minor league roster.

In his place, they have drafted Kevin Phillips, who was the Smithers to Peter Crouch's Mr Burns during their time at the South Hamptons. They've also traded for Patrik Berger, who sounds a bit tasty.

They also managed to get Euro Series finalist Milan Baros from the Liverpool Reds (or was it Liverpool Baros from Milan AC?).

Key kicker – Wilfred Bouma: The Holiday Homes' first soccer woman, so it will be interesting to see how she gets on. Her ball control is second to none, but she has problems with spacial awareness and eye-to-foot coordination.

Worst kicker – Steve Davis: One of the Aston Holiday Homes most experienced kickers, having been world champion seven times in a funny sport called snooker, which is a mixture of billiards and math. But can the Golden Nugget conquer another sport? I'm thinking he'll be like Michael Jordan in baseball, rather than basketball.

The Everton Stickies

They were the surprise package last series, finishing fourth when many expected them to finish fourth from bottom in the EPL. Their most famous player is called Duncan Ferguson. His nickname is Big Dunk, which is the name of the bullying technique he used at school when he used to dunk the heads of the geeks in the bathroom stalls and flush.

Despite finishing so high last series, they traded for a lot of kickers this summer, including Matteo Ferrari. To me, he just looks flash, but he is very quick.

Still, Wayne Roonaldo roots for the Stickies, so they can't be all bad.

Key kicker – Andy Vandermeyde: Drafted from International Milan, he has a great pedigree, but then so did Lassie and he never made it in the EPL. Unfortunately, being a middleman for the Stickies is likely to involve craning you neck as the ball flies high over your head.

Worst kicker – James Beattie: Pop says there's an old soccer adage that says a good kicker doesn't become a bad kicker overnight. James Beattie is the exception that proves the rule.

The Boltonians

The team from the posh northern boarding school look strong again this series with Argentinian head coach Sam Allardyce (pronounced Al-ar-dee-chey) on the sidelines.

Pop says they are known for their long-ball soccer, which I think is a reference to rugby soccer, which is played with a 'longer' egg-shaped ball, like they use in football.

Their stepoveringest kicker is called Jay-Jay Okocha, the man so good they named him twice. I've not heard anyone saying that about Eric Djemba-Djemba.

Key kicker – Kevin Nolan: One of the top score-kicking middlemen in the EPL, Nolan's no-nonsense approach typifies the Boltonians. He's often in the mood for dancing, romancing and giving it all tonight.

Worst kicker – El Hadji Diouf: Wispy wideout who is so

lightweight that he gets shoved to the ground by a light breeze. Also has a saliva problem.

The Middle Borough

This inner-city London franchise has made big trades this summer, with former Manchester assistant head coach Steve McLaren only drafting players with odd names. So in come Aiyegbeni Yakubu and Emanuel Pogatetz, whose names get more points for Scrabble than any other soccer player.

They have also re-signed Massimo Maccarone after he spent a year in the Austrian capital of Siena. I'm sure the Italian will be looking for a pizza the action. I reckon he'll win lots of penne-ties and be able to gnocchi the ball into the goal.

I think they might have made a mistake when they decided to draft former Liverpool Reds fashion guru Abel Xavier, along with his brother Cain. I don't think they get on very well and that could end badly. Abel Xavier looks far bigger than the last time I saw him. He must have been working out.

Key kicker – Mark Viduka/Jimmy Hasselbank: I couldn't separate them, as they are so similar. On their day, they are magnificent score-kicking machines. When they are off-form, they are so lethargic that they get the coach to bring out a couple of La-Z Boy Chairs into the middle of the gridiron and they watch the game from there.

Worst kicker – Malcolm Christie: Famous as being the former drugstore shelf-stacker that made it in the EPL. However, he has re-trained as a physio and is spending all his time in the treatment room at the moment.

The Newcastle Stripers

The Newcastle Stripers should have more money to spend than any other franchise. They sell so many jerseys that they actually made a design out of the barcode to make it easier for the megastore manager.

But they haven't made too many big trades, bringing in just three kickers. There's Scott Parker from the London Chelseas, Irish international Albert O'Looque and Emma Ray

Belozoglu, the first female soccer player to make it to the EPL, known simply as Em Ray.

Key kicker – Alan Shearer: In his 40s, but still kicking plenty of scores. Someone once referred to him as Mary Poppins, which I think is unfair. With Mary Poppins, it takes a spoonful of sugar to make something go down. Shearer does that with an elbow to the face.

Worst kicker – Lee Bowyer: He reckons he is one of the best kickers at the franchise, but then he was branded a liar by a judge, so I doubt it. He had a scrap with team-mate Keiron Dyer last year, but fighting team-mates never did Roy Keano any harm.

MID-DIVISION NO-HOPERS

Blackburn Pyros

The Blackburn Pyros, a team from a northern prison, have been adding more and more violent anti-social personalities to their side this year, drafting Craig Bellamy and Robbie Savage.

They are head coached by Manchester Hall of Famer Mark Hughes, who is nicknamed Sparky as he used to earn extra money mending the wiring at the Nike Trafford Ballpark. At least that explains how he got his hair like that.

London Arsenals youngster David Bentley has been given 12 months for joyriding in a golf cart and he has permission from his franchise to kick for the Pyros this series.

Key kicker – Brad Friedel: Super American goaltender, almost as good as Timmy Howard, but a little inconsistent nowadays. Some days, you just know that no one will ever get the ball past him into the scoring zone. Other days, you wonder if he's actually made of Swiss cheese.

Worst kicker – Robbie Savage: Currently with the Blackburn Pyros for stealing Jessica Simpson's hair, the middleman specializes in really annoying everyone else. His best moves are flicking opponents' ears and tapping them on the shoulder and running away. I don't think anyone has ever seen him kick a soccer ball.

Fulham Fayeds

Originally a franchise based in Egypt, the Fulham Fayeds moved to this country but found they were unable to get a British passport and might have to move back to Egypt sometime soon.

 They dealt goaltender Eddie Vandersar to Manchester, so might have problems stopping points against them. They haven't really replaced him yet, but should be able to get a big discount if they find a new goaltender at Harrods.

They did draft Tony Warner, a goaltender from the Cardiff Casseroles, who looks like David James, both in appearance and talent. That's why I said they haven't really replaced Vandersar properly.

Key kicker – Carlos Bocanegra: Fearless left cornerback who is being tipped to be one of the best kickers in his position. What do you mean you haven't heard of him?

Worst kicker – Tomasz Radzinski: The man with the irrelevant 'Z' in his name came with a big reputation, but his six EPL scores is a pretty poor return. He comes from Canada, so he speaks bad English and has a fairly substantial inferiority complex, eh.

Pompeii Pompeys

The oldest club in the British league, the Pompeii Pompeys date back to ancient times.

Head coach Alan Perrin, nicknamed 'Reg' because of his collection of license plates, has been busy in the trade market this summer, drafting Sander Westerveld and Andy O'Brien.

They also brought in Laurent Robert, who reminds me of the moody French exchange student that stayed in our house last year who refused to talk or shower for the whole week.

Key kicker – Lomano LuaLua: The most unpredictable kicker in the EPL. Capable of slaloming runs that end in a score, but often he does the slaloming run, just without the ball. Has the best celebration around, with his quadruple front flip. It's just a shame we don't see it more often.

Worst kicker – Svetolslav Todorov: A very competitive category. Not that he is a bad kicker as such, it's just that I'm not entirely sure he's ever kicked before. In fact, there is a small chance that he is a figment of the Pompeys' imagination. I've never seen him on the roster.

Charlton Addicts

Apparently, the Charlton Addicts have been in the EPL for a long time, but have never been anywhere near the play-offs or the demotion places. They're a bit like Pop's strange brother, my Uncle Jimmy – no one actually likes or dislikes him. We all humor him . . . he means no harm after all.

The entire team is from the Outreach program who bravely battle their serious habits to play their home-fields in the Valley, which Pop says is in the English city of Wales. Danny Murphy, for example, is addicted to sniffing gruyere and has to go to Cheese Anonymous every week.

They should be much, much better this series, having drafted Manchester's American wonderkid Jonathan Spector, who will instantly improve their roster. They have also traded for a Bent kicker. I can't remember his name.

Key kicker – Jay Bothroyd: Drafted on a no-fee relocation
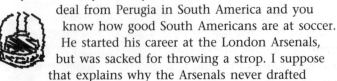 deal from Perugia in South America and you know how good South Americans are at soccer. He started his career at the London Arsenals, but was sacked for throwing a strop. I suppose that explains why the Arsenals never drafted Laurent Robert.

Worst kicker – Jason Euell: Pronounced 'You'll' as in 'You'll never kick a score again' or 'You'll wonder how he cost 8.2 million English dollars.'

Birmingham Bullets

Former Manchester middleman Nicky Butt has just been drafted by the Birmingham Bullets, the British soccer arm of the Alabama franchise. He had a terrible time at the Newcastle Stripers, a team he only joined because his dyslexic agent told him he'd be playing with some Newcastle Strippers.

Another new kicker for them is Walter Pandiani and, because he is known as 'The Rifle', I can only assume he is American. Surely combining the Rifle and the Bullets will have a deadly effect.

Former Liverpool Reds offenser Emile Heskey is currently at the Bullets, proving that top-quality kickers can fall over for small franchises as well as big ones.

Key kicker – Mikael Forssell: Drafted from the London Chelseas, claiming him on squatters' rights after having him for two years before then. He is the highest-scoring albino in the history of the EPL.

Worst kicker – Jermaine Pennant: Not a bad kicker, just a bit out of control. Was loaned to the Blackburn Pyros for a month or so after a motor vehicle incident that featured a lamp post, a policeman, a false name and not being able to read.

DEMOTION FAVORITES

The Western Bromwiches

The Western Bromwiches avoided demotion to the minor leagues in the final regular series game in May, mainly inspired by former Manchester whizzkid Keiron Richardson. Sir Fergie noticed that and re-signed the Britain star this summer.

They might be in trouble without him. What was head coach Bryan Robson thinking trading him back to us? He's an idiot . . . thank God he's got no connections with a great franchise like Manchester.

One top star they have is goaltender Chris Kirkland, who they drafted from the Liverpool Reds' minor league team, the Liverpool Intensive Cares.

Key kicker – Zoltan Gera: Not only the Western

Bromwiches' top kicker, but a world-class psychic, who made Tom Hanks 'Big' in the 1988 movie.

Worst kicker – N. Kanu: I don't think he's that bad, but the fans hate him. Not only do they boo him whenever he does anything, but they also call him N. 'Wankwo' Kanu.

The Wigan Warriors

I'm sorry, I don't really know anything about them, so I've had a look on the internet. Their star man is called Andrew Farrell, although I think he may have left to join the union (does that mean the Professional Soccer Players Association? He's not planning to go on strike, is he?).

Even though they have a plan to get three points for every score, they are certainties to be demoted. There is no way that they will win even one game, let alone survive in the EPL. You can quote me on that.

Key kicker – No idea.

Worst kicker – Where do I begin? Jason Roberts won't kick many scores. My guess is that head coach Paul Jewell won't last until November.

The Western Hammers

I'm not sure why everyone thinks they are certainties for demotion, considering they were play-off champions last series. That makes them a big threat to Manchester.

Manchester fans have a good reason to hate the Western Hammers – they were the fanchise that first brought Ferdinand Rio to the EPL from Brazil, where he used to play soccer on gravel fields with no shoes on.

New star Yossi Benayoun could prove a big hit for the franchise, after being drafted from the Israeli side he owns, Yossi's Giants.

Key kicker – Teddy Sheringham: Despite being in his 50s, the former Manchester star is still a roster regular at the Western Hammers. He doesn't have any pace now, but then Pop tells me he never did.

Worst kicker – Anton Rio: Younger brother of Manchester's Ferdinand Rio. All the reports I've read say he's not as good as Ferdinand, which means I can't ever fathom how bad he must be.

August 4 – Manchester lose another great player

Sir Fergie has done it again. Just when I get confident with the way this series is shaping up, he goes and trades another international kicker.

Phil Neville, the younger brother of Manchester prefect Gary, has been traded to the Everton Stickies for 3.5 million English dollars.

Neville must be a great player. He was part of the Manchester roster that won the Euro Series and he has 52 caps for Britain (I think he gets a cap from Sven Eriksson every time he tells on a team-mate). That makes him better than Roy Keano who was cut for the Euro Series final and has 52 less Britain appearances.

Yet once again, Sir Fergie has misjudged the situation and dealt him out. I'm sure it can't be long before Super Malcolm realizes this and replaces him with Sir Phelan, the current practice roster head coach – and the winningest coach at the franchise.

August 7 – London Chelseas top Opening Week EPL standings

The EPL series got underway in traditional fashion as last year's top two franchises met on Opening Day.

The London Chelseas moved straight back to the top of the standings as they kicked two scores to the London Arsenals' one in the Western English city of Wales. Manchester are a disappointing 10th.

Didier Drogba, an offenser from the Coat D'Ivoire, a chilly seaside resort in southern France, was the MVP with both points, while Chesc Fabregas, the London Arsenals' 13-year-old Doogie Howser MD (MD stands for middleman), kicked their score.

So here are the EPL standings after Week One:

	W	L	T	GB
London Chelseas	1	0	0	–
Aston Holiday Homes	0	0	0	0.5
Birmingham Bullets	0	0	0	0.5
Blackburn Pyros	0	0	0	0.5
Boltonians	0	0	0	0.5
Charlton Addicts	0	0	0	0.5
Everton Stickies	0	0	0	0.5
Fulham Fayeds	0	0	0	0.5
Liverpool Reds	0	0	0	0.5
Manchester	0	0	0	0.5
Newcastle Stripers	0	0	0	0.5
Pompeii Pompeys	0	0	0	0.5
Sunderland	0	0	0	0.5
The Middle Borough	0	0	0	0.5
Tott Nam	0	0	0	0.5
Western Bromwiches	0	0	0	0.5
Western Hammers	0	0	0	0.5
Wigan Warriors	0	0	0	0.5
London Arsenals	0	1	0	1

But I don't think this is very fair. The London Chelseas are already one win ahead of all the other teams, even though they were the best by a long way last series. Why should they get an extra game? I assume it's a bonus because they won the pennant, but it still makes it harder for Manchester.

August 8 — Brazil star Rio Grand after new deal

Brazilian defenseman Ferdinand Rio has inked a new deal to keep him at the Manchester franchise until 2009.

The former Leeds Enrons back was labelled 'greedy', I

think because he refused to share his potato chips with others on the roster.

Manchester fans jeered him during the pre-series matches, despite Rio's insistence that they were Original-flavored Pringles and that 'Once you pop, you can't stop.'

But Rio has put an end to the problems by agreeing the new contract, worth a very reasonable 100,000 English dollars per week. The franchise hope that this is the end of the matter, although Wayne Roonaldo is said to still be upset, as that's his favorite flavor and he only wanted a handful.

Although that's good news, there's also some bad news for Manchester. That idiot Sir Fergie has traded Kleberson back to Brazilian side Besiktas.

It was bad enough national franchise star kicker Phil Neville leaving, but this is a World Cup winner! You only get the chance to win the World Cup once every year, so you have to be good.

Yet, according to Sir Fergie, he is happy with a middleman line-up of Quinton Fortune and Liam Miller, who is so anonymous, he couldn't even get picked out of a police line-up, let alone a soccer one.

August 9 — Glazers get to see Manchester play (I wish I could)

I'm so jealous . . . the Glazer triplets will watch their first regular series Manchester game tonight as we play in a Euro Series qualifier.

Malcolm's three mini-mes will be at the Nike Trafford Ballpark as Manchester face a Hungarian team whose head coach is a Chinese woman called Deborah Chen.

There are still some tickets available for the Euro Series clash, which is great news! It means that there is space for fans like me, who started rooting for Manchester when Glazer took over.

Head coach Sir Fergie has asked fans to welcome the

Glazers and show them what makes the stadium a 'truly electric place'. Let's hope none of them take it the wrong way and hook up the Glazers' seats in the bleachers like electric chairs!

August 10 — Manchester 3–0 Deborah Chen XI

Manchester started the series as they finished the last one – with no trophies and the Nike Trafford Ballpark half empty. But it's looking more positive now, after Rude and the Roonaldo brothers took Deborah Chen's XI apart.

There are some protests against the Glazer triplets at the game, as about 100 fans turned up almost five minutes late, having only spent 83 English dollars in the Megastore beforehand. I'm sure the Glazers will be concerned.

But on the gridiron, everything went perfectly. Wayne Roonaldo kicked Manchester into the lead after just seven minutes, and then turned quarterback to set up scores for his brother Cristiano and Rude Nistelrooy.

Deborah Chen had coached her franchise to the pennant in Hungary and that's very impressive, but how come she qualifies for the Euro Series? Hungary isn't in Europe! Next, they will allow Russian teams into the competition.

Manchester is now virtually guaranteed a place in the Euro Series first round. Although this was the third round, despite being our first round, so we are actually close to getting into the fourth round, which is a divisional format. It's very confusing! You Brits need lessons on how to label your pennants!

August 12 — Introducing the Everton Stickies

It's time! After a summer of waiting, Manchester's EPL series gets underway.

We travel north to play the Everton Stickies, the former franchise of Wayne Roonaldo. It's going to be a very tough game. They finished just one position behind us in the standings last year.

Defenseman Michael Silvester claims the entire Manchester roster is hungry. I suppose it's because Ferdinand Rio is still eating all the Pringles.

So who are the kickers against us on Opening Day? Here is a guide to the Stickies.

Phil Neville

He'll be playing against his big brother Gary for the first time since they were both Hall Monitors at Manchester Junior High and because of this I can see us getting a few 12-yard kick-ball punishments. And we won't let Paul Scholes take them this time.

David Weir

He is the Weir that is charged with stopping the flow of Manchester's score-getting river. He is a giant defenseman with one of the squarest side-parting hairstyles in soccer.

Alessandra Pistone

In the Everton Stickies defense, Alessandra is the Dyke to David's Weir.

August 13 — Everton Stickies 0–2 Manchester

Manchester moved top of the EPL after an Opening Day triumph over the Everton Stickies. We moved one and oh and top the standings at 9am Eastern Time.

Rude Nistelrooy hit the go-ahead score inside the two-minute warning at the end of the first half, kicking home Jono Shea's centre.

Then, when Everton's thuggish defender Joseph (nicknamed 'Yobbo') made a mistake, Wayne Roonaldo moved Manchester two scores up.

Despite the win, there was yet another howler from Sir Ferguson, who cut Cristiano Roonaldo for the game.

I heard the wideout kicked a good game in the Euro Series on Tuesday and I thought he should have been in the starting roster today, especially as he grew up with his brother Wayne just outside the Everton Stickies Stadium. But the head coach disagreed and played the Korean Megastore manager Park Ji-Sung instead.

I suppose Park will be in the starting roster for most of the road games, while when we are playing at the Nike Trafford Ballpark, he will have to spend his time selling shirts and telling the spotty 15-year-olds behind the counter how to use a cash machine.

August 14 — EPL XIV takes off in style

What an Opening Day weekend for EPL XIV!

The London Chelseas beat the Wigan Warriors when Herman Crespo picked up where he left off last series, kicking a point-winning score in the last seconds of regulation time.

The Warriors thought they had won the game when Damien Francis's header hit the horizontal bar and went over, but they had to be reminded you don't get points in soccer for doing that.

The London Arsenals started their series with a win over 10-man Newcastle, for whom Jermaine Jenas was ejected by the podgy referee for being too lanky.

Meanwhile, the Liverpool Reds suffered a European hangover following their Euro Series qualifier as they struggled to a zip-zip tie with the Middle Borough.

I read that they always suffer from Euro Series hangovers, which must be because they have too much liquor on the plane ride home. Although that seems a bit odd, as Pop tells me that British Airways have problems doing food and drink on their flights nowadays.

August 16 — Smith turns down Britain call

Manchester offenser Alan Smith is in a bit of trouble with the Soccer Association.

Smith, who played 13 times for Britain while at the London Arsenals before he shrunk eight inches and got traded to Manchester, claimed he would rather play for our practice squad than for his country.

It seems a strange decision, but I can fully understand it. Having played under Sir Fergie for a year, he must be desperate to kick for a good head coach and this is his one chance to be coached by Sir Michael Phelan, Manchester's winningest coach.

Britain are playing in Denmark in a qualifying game for World Cup XVIII.

Meanwhile, Manchester legend Timmy Howard is in action as Team USA faces the might of Trinidad and Tobago. They are two countries playing together, so it will be a tough game, although Pop says all their kickers are too busy watching something called The Ashes.

He says it is a cricket game, which gones on for ages and yet no one wins. A bit like the War on Terror, then.

August 17 — Roonaldo turned down the London Chelseas to kick with brother

Wayne Roonaldo has revealed that he turned down the chance to be traded by the London Chelseas to join Manchester.

Our star offenser said that he did not want to live in London, preferring to live near the Nike Trafford Ballpark on the outskirts of the city. I think his main reason might be that there is a far higher percentage of women in their 50s near our Ballpark than near the London Chelseas'.

Wayne, who admitted he was also keen to kick for the same franchise as his brother Cristiano, claimed that Gary Neville and Roy Keano have helped him to become the player he is.

I presume Neville has helped him with his consistency, while Keano must have been influential in developing his violent, petulant side.

August 18 — Manchester goaltender lets down his country

Maybe Sir Fergie isn't so bad after all.

Britain got a Danish pasting last night as they were beaten four to one in a qualifying game for World Cup XVIII. The man most at fault was goaltender David James.

I looked up who he played for and I couldn't believe it. It's us – Manchester! I never knew he was on our roster. At least Sir Fergie can see that he's no good and has demoted him to our practice squad.

With the score at zip-zip, James jogged to the 30-yard line to block a Hail Mary pass, but completely missed it and watched the rest unfold on his butt, as Charlton Addicts line sprinter Dennis Rommedahl tucked the ball into the score-zone.

 JD Tomasson, an offenser named after his favorite drink – Tomasson's Tropical Fruit Crush – added a second when London Chelseas cornerback Glenn Johnson was struck by a bout of narcolepsy, while Michael Graveyard made it three scores.

Wayne Roonaldo, who had spent the game sitting on the midway line cross-legged out of boredom, kicked the definition of a consolation score in the last minute, but there was still time for Soren Larsen to add a fourth score and heap more humiliation on to Britain.

So however bad Sir Fergie is, at least he is not Sven Eriksson. Then Manchester would really be in trouble.

Meanwhile, Team USA beat both Trinidad AND Tobago, thanks to a single score by Fulham Fayeds offenser Brian McBride.

Now that David Bellion has been traded to the Western Hammers, Manchester could do a lot worse than draft

McBride in his place. He has 20 scores for Team USA, which is more than either Rude Nistelrooy or Wayne Roonaldo have for their countries.

August 19 – Roonaldo and his learnt lessons

Wayne Roonaldo has admitted he was embarrassed by Britain's four to one loss to Denkark and has vowed to make sure it never happens again.

He said he hates losing by one score, so losing by three is horrible. Luckily, with Manchester being such a top franchise, at least that's never going to happen. In all the time I've been a Manchester fan (and it's a long time now . . . almost three months), we haven't lost by more than one score!

'It's an important part of my learning curve,' said Wayne, adding it to his lessons learnt list – along with make sure your girlfriend can shop as often as she likes, don't go to massage parlors and don't drink a beauty potion with your friend Donkey to impress your fiancée, Princess Fiona.

But I think we should all get behind Wayne. He is a person who doesn't know the meaning of the word *fear*. Or the word *car*, or *dog* or a huge number of other words.

Still I can confidently say that Manchester will never lose by four to one in any game against anyone. Not the London Chelseas, not Realmadrid. Not even the Middle Borough.

Next up for Britain is a game against Wales. How can we be playing Wales? It's just a city in England . . . how can it have its own country team? If Wales have a team, then what next? Scotland will want its own national team as well!

Meanwhile, back in the EPL, the London Chelseas have strengthened their roster yet again, adding African star Michael Essien to their starting positions.

The middleman was traded for Tiago and a shedload of used 5 English dollar notes from French franchise the Lyon

Tigersandbearsohmys. He excelled in the Euro Series last year, kicking five scores in 10 games as the Tigersandbearsohmys lost in the quarter-finals of the pennant.

That's the last thing we need. The London Chelseas are already better than us and now they've brought in a kicker that Manchester wanted to replace Roy Keano. Our only hope is that Essien does the psycho bit of Keano, without the top middleman part.

20 August — Manchester 1—0 Aston Holiday Homes

Manchester went back to the top of the EPL standings as they moved to two and oh with a win over the Aston Holiday Homes.

Rude Nistelrooy kicked the only score of the game, faucetting home a center from replacement Cristiano Roonaldo in the second period.

Holiday Homes goaltender Thomas Sorensen, who had just returned from Denmark's stunning win over Britain, spent half his time making wonderful blocks and the other half laughing hysterically at all the British kickers like Paul Scholes and Darren Fletcher.

His opposite number Eddie Vandersar, meanwhile, was a spectator for the entire game, so much so that at one stage a steward threatened to eject him from the ground if he didn't show a valid ticket for the game.

According to the report from the British Broadcasting Company, the only thing that shone out early on was the industry of Park Ji-Sung, so he must have been selling shirts particularly quickly before the game.

August 22 — Drogba provides Zidane-like genius

Yeah! Manchester is already a win ahead of the London Arsenals following Week Two in the EPL.

But the bad news is that the London Chelseas are getting

better and better. In fact, they are getting so good that they are inventing new ways to get a score.

On Sunday, French offenser Didier Drogba got the point-winning score, when he preteneded to miscontrol the ball, only to cleverly knock the ball past London Arsenals goaltender Jens Lehmann with his knee. I don't know how you stop a trick play like that.

Pop says that last week, Drogba played against a man called Zidane Zidane, who was voted the world's MVP, and he must have picked up a few special moves.

The rest of the game was spent with the London Chelseas kicking the ball as far out of the stadium as they could to waste time. One ball got so far, it is still going and was last seen rolling around a roundabout in Milton Keynes.

Meanwhile, Sir Fergie revealed he is still looking for one last kicker to make sure Manchester finish as high as second in the pennant race. One player I read he is interested in is Ayax big man Daniel de Ridder. Wayne Roonaldo was a bit worried by this, because he overheard Sir Fergie telling the GM: 'We need to get Ridder the fat youngster.'

August 23 — Smith the new Keano

Alan Smith will play as a deep middleman when Manchester face the Deborah Chen XI on Wednesday.

Sir Fergie has been furious with the displays of Roy 'Keane' Keano and has decided to cut the Englishman for the upcoming match.

Smith, whose nickname is 'Smudger' as his handwriting looks like that of an eight-year-old, will play the holding role, which will involve him trying to hold on to his position in the team without being ejected . . . something he has only done a couple of times in his career.

Pop says Smith has a few similarities with Keano. Both have psychotic tendencies and have a really bad haircut.

Wayne Roonaldo's failure to get a score against the Aston Holiday Homes means that he will be replaced by his brother Cristiano, while Park Ji-Sung will be left at home to sell more shirts, so veteran wideout Ryan Giggs will kick.

August 24 — CSKA clinch Euro Series title

CSKA Sophia are officially the best team in the whole of Europe after getting a win against Euro Series winners the Liverpool Reds.

The French Championship team, who was named after their film star head coach Sophia Loren, won one to zip at Ann's Field to take the Euro Series title belt.

That's definitely a good thing for Manchester. We know that the Liverpool Reds are a better franchise than us, but maybe – just maybe – we can beat CSKA Sophia. I mean, how good can a team coached by a woman be? Especially one whose only real soccer experience was in a film called *La Ciociara*, a biopic about the famous Italian defenseman Mario Ciociara.

By the way, how do you pronounce that name – CSKA Sophia? It it Kuss-car?

August 25 — Deborah Chen XI 0–3 Manchester

Gabriel Heinze kicked two head-scores as Manchester beat the Deborah Chen XI three to zip for a second time in two weeks.

Argentinia star Heinze is normally a defensive end, but with Manchester struggling for scores last series, maybe they should play him as an offenser in the future.

I'm a bit confused by this game though. We beat them in the Euro Series last time and knocked them out of the competition, so this game can't have been for that pennant.

Everyone else played an EPL game, so I think this must have been an EPL game. It seems Deborah Chen has moved her franchise to the EPL. Still, that's good, because we are now three and oh, and only the London Chelseas have managed that.

Meanwhile, the London Arsenals unveiled a new scoring sensation last night as young Frenchman Pascal Cygan got two in their win over the Fulham Fayeds. I wish Sir Fergie could find prospects as good as Cygan for Manchester.

August 26 — Manchester agree Euro Series Division

Manchester has announced they are to join the Euro Series this year.

I think we are still going to be in the EPL as well, so the kickers will have to do a lot of kicking in the next year.

The other franchises that have agreed to be in our division are Real Villa of Spain, the Lille Savages and the Ben Fica XI.

It means Manchester will get a chance to look at Europe's top offenser Diego Forlan, who kicks for the Real Villa. I think this will be the first time he has played in Britain, so let's hope he catches Sir Fergie's eye.

I don't think it will be a problem for Manchester, as we have Rude 'The Van' Nistelrooy, who is one of the top score-kickers in the country. He is in such good form this series, he has as many goals in the EPL as Arsenals superstar Pascal Cygan, so he must be good.

August 28 — Newcastle Stripers 0–2 Manchester

Manchester survived a terrible performance at the Newcastle Stripers to move to four and oh in the EPL.

Having already got wins against the Stickies, Holiday Homes and Deborah Chen XI in the competition, scores kicked by Wayne Roonaldo and Rude Nistelrooy were enough to continue their perfect start to the series.

But the game, played at St James' Park, next to Buckingham Palace in London, should have been much easier. The Stripers have yet to notch a score, while our defensemen have not given up one, so it should have been much more convincing than we made it.

Wayne Roonaldo took advantage of a defense error by centre-back brothers Jean and Alain Boumsong to thump the ball past goaltender Che Gueven, who is clearly better at starting Cuban revolutions than stopping scores.

Then Nistelrooy added a second inside the two-minute warning for his fourth one-yard score of the series.

Park Ji-Sung only came on for five minutes at the end of the game as he spent the rest of the time on a fact-finding mission, discovering how the Stripers manage to sell so many jerseys.

Even more strange is that although they sell a lot of their uniforms, everyone takes them off and watches the match topless, despite the cold British weather.

August 30 — Manchester miss out on Michael

Manchester have missed out on another Britain star after the Newcastle Stripers drafted Michael Owen in a 30 million English dollars deal.

Pop says the offenser spent much of last series warming the bench for Realmadrid, which involves rubbing it for 15 minutes during the half-time show to make it comfy for the players that were actually named as replacements.

Owen was always going to have a hard time breaking into the starting roster for the Portugalese side, with stars like Roonaldo, Raul and Rob Inyo in front of him.

They must be stars, because like Madonna and Cher, they only go by their first name and you must be good to get away with that. With the exception of Doriva. And Tiffany, obviously.

Owen was born in Wales and has 70 caps for Britain. Because of this, I think he will be ineligible for the regional exhibition game between Wales and the Rest of Britain this weekend. I'm already confused about why this game is being played. It's not like Britain have ever played London, which is the same thing.

August 31 — Fight back with our Glazer T-shirts

I thought this had all gone away, but apparently, a minority of Manchester fans are to protest against Super Malcolm Glazer.

They are all planning to wear 'Glazer Out' T-shirts to an upcoming EPL game, after one supporter was told to take his T-shirt off last week.

I'm not sure how they are planning to do this, as I thought that all 'true' fans opposed to the Glaz-meister had already burnt their series tickets. Still, it's not going to be very effective. I'll have to ask Pop, but I'm fairly sure you Brits didn't overcome the Nazis by wearing 'Hitler Out' jerseys.

Still we need to fight for the pro-Glazer majority. Make sure that, whenever you go to the Nike Trafford Ballpark, you wear your Glazer T-shirts from the Manchester Buccaneers Megastore.

 ## September 1 — Trade deadline review

When Manchester drafted Eddie Vandersar, I thought it would make the defense steady but I was worried that it wasn't going to help us get scores, which is where we needed help.

Local rivals the London Arsenals also traded for a goaltender, but they went one better and got Martin Poom on Wednesday. He is not only a goaltender who has played over 754 times for his country, but is also a talented offenser, having hit crucial scores for his franchise. He would have been perfect for us.

Meanwhile, Tott Nam traded for Newcastle Stripers Jermaine Jenas, adding him to a list of middlemen so big, I can only imagine head coach Martin Jol is planning to open an eBay shop.

They also added Grzegorz Rasiak from Welsh side the Derby Sheep. I'm not sure how you pronounce his first name, but Pop says you can only say it correctly if you've had a tracheotomy.

Elsewhere, Manchester feeder franchise PSG Eindhoven, who we've drafted Park, Nistelrooy and Heinze from, have traded British singer Michael Ball for all their pre-game entertainment. He'll be belting out 'Love Changes Everything' to all the Hollandish fans on a weekly basis.

And finally the Pompeii Pompeys brought in Irishman Darry O'Silva, the brother of the London Arsenals' Gilbert. It was a day of trading that Wall Street would be proud of.

September 2 — Glazer directs money to roster affairs

Malcolm Glazer has started to make back the money he spent on buying Manchester.

The multimillionaire businessman has come up with the brilliant idea of sacking 25 of Manchester's support staff.

Gone are some of the ticket agents and, with the level of customer service you get in Britain, the only surprise is that they weren't sacked far sooner. Besides, tickets sell out weeks in advance, so the agents are just telling people to go away.

Vera the tea-maid has also left, to be replaced by a Flavia automatic drinks machine. This has two advantages, the first being that it makes far better tea and the second that it doesn't insist on telling you about how clever its grandchildren are or how noisy the neighbours are.

I think this is a great idea and really explains how Super Malcolm became a multimillionaire in the first place. Getting rid of 25 staff means we can afford to give Ferdinand Rio the 200,000 English dollars a week that he wants and the roster is improved. How can you argue with that?

September 4 — Wales 0–1 Rest of Britain

A score from the London Chelseas' Ashley Cole was enough to give the Rest of Britain side a one-zip win over the City of Wales XI.

In the nation-on-nation exhibition kick contest, Wales didn't even see the soccer ball in the first period, with the Rest of Britain roster acting like my school-pal Chuck, who won't let anyone else play with his balls. Although the principal sometimes insists on playing with them.

But in the second period, Cole produced one of his trademark scores. Ninety-three percent of his scores for the London Chelseas are ricochets off an opponent's ass and he transferred his form to the nation-on-nation stage, squeezing his kick into the score-zone off the rear of Wales defenseman Gabi Dannydon.

Next up, the Wales kickers swap sides to join the Rest of Britain side – so Michael Owen can return to the roster – as they take on Norn Iron, playing at Windsor Park, just outside the castle.

5 September — My ideal job!

I've been writing this website about Manchester for four months now and I think I know as much about our soccer franchise as anyone.

So I was really excited when a kind person told me of an ideal job for me (I know I'm only in 7th grade, but I read at a 9th-grade level). Below is my application to become the new editor of the Manchester Matchday program, as seen on the website of a jobs newspaper called the *Guardian*.

Applications go to a place called Teddington, which I looked up and is in South-West London, so it can't be too far from the Nike Trafford Ballpark. I'll let you know how I get on.

Roswell P Shambling
4283263 *NSync Street
Fort Myers, FL 33901

September 6, 2005

Haymarket Network
38–42 Hampton Road
Teddington
Middlesex TW11 0JE

Dear Mr Glazer,

I would like to apply for the position of Matchday
Program Editor for the Manchester soccer roster.

I have a great amount of experience, having been writing
and editing a website on the franchise, which was named
Yahoo's Website of the Week and has been praised by the
Guardian, When Saturday Comes and Zoo Weekly (*http://
spaces.msn.com/members/ManchesterBuccaneers/*). It has
proved extremely popular and I feel I could bring the same
kind of following to the program.

I currently live in the USA and am a huge Manchester
fan. I have been for ages now . . . almost four months. I
started rooting for them once Malcolm Glazer became the
new leader and am the Glaz-meister's biggest fan. My
favorite player is Roy Keano and I just can't understand
why he has never been picked for the England side.

The Manchester fans seem to be very much against Super
Malcolm, but I think I can help write articles that will help
them get behind the franchise. For example, I have written a
song about Super Malcolm and I think if we could get the
crowd singing it, it would be great.

I have an in-depth knowledge about Manchester. For other
soccer, I know a bit and my Pop is teaching me as much as
possible. For example, I know that the London Arsenals
have seen their Irish midfield partnership of Paddy Vieira
and Gilbert O'Silva broken up when Vieira joined Uventus
in Italy.

Although I am currently in the USA, I am hoping to

move to London to live right by the Manchester Ballpark and would really like to work with my favorite kickers.

I look forward to hearing from you.

Yours Sincerely
Roswell P Shambling

ROSWELL P SHAMBLING
Resumé

Address: 4283263 *NSync Street, Fort Myers, FL 33901
Date of Birth: April 6, 1993
Nationality: American

EDUCATION
English A – Top of my grade
History D – Top of my grade
Math Geometry B+, Algebra X
Geography N/A

RELEVANT EXPERIENCE
May 2005–present: Managing Editor, Manchester Buccaneers site
http://spaces.msn.com/members/ManchesterBuccaneers/
Responsibilities include:
– Creating the award-winning website spreading the word of Manchester's soccer franchise around the world.
– In charge of writing daily news and opinion articles and publishing them on the website.
– Launched an eBusiness, selling Manchester Buccaneers-branded merchandise, including T-shirts, mugs and hotpants.

May 2005–present: Manchester soccer franchise fan
– In-depth knowledge of all the Manchester kickers, even the rubbish ones (like Quinton Fortune).
– Love of the new regime, Malcolm Glazer in particular.

QUALIFICATIONS
Yahoo Website of the Week
Fully competent with a wide range of computer programs

100-yard swimming badge
NRA Marksmanship Qualification
Abraham C. Myers Junior High Talent Show – 2nd place

INTERESTS
Heavy rock music (such as Maroon 5 and Hootie and the Blowfish)
Football
Soccer

Roswell R Shambling, September 2005

September 8 – Humbling defeat for Britain

Team Britain succumbed to a humiliating defeat last night.

Sven Eriksson's men were beaten by a team called Norn Iron, a makeshift team from a city in the north of Ireland that didn't even include a lot of the best players from the country, who were playing for their proper national side against France.

(Incidentally, in that Ireland v France game, France turned up with only 10 players, so Ireland had to lend Paddy Vieira to France for the match to make it fair.)

The team England lost to were a group of journeymen who play for minor-league English franchises like the Plymouth Pirates and Motherwell Mothers. I believe some of them had never seen a soccer ball before last Monday. A couple were only seven years old and one was a pygmy.

Leeds Enrons offenser David Healy kicked the only score, picking up a slide-ruler pass from Steven Davis and thumping the ball past the helpless goaltender Paul Robinson, who had come all the way from Ramsey Street, Australia for the game.

Still at least it was only an exhibition game and wasn't a World Cup XVIII preliminary round or anything important. That would have been really embarrassing.

September 9 – Roonaldo fury at flash Beckham

Wayne Roonaldo was true to his earlier words that he hated losing by screaming abust at whoever came near him.

Earlier, head coach Sven Eriksson had blamed Roonaldo for the defeat, claiming his 'stupid challenge' ruined Britain's spirit. Yet he somehow failed to mention that the Sir Fergie-like poor selection and under-motivated kickers may have had a part to play in it!

After that, Eriksson then went on to blame Roonaldo's quick change of direction for causing Hurricane Katrina and his enormous weight for the tsunami in December.

During the game, Roonaldo let loose what the reports in the press called 'a ferocious tirade' or a 'verbal volley' at David Beckham, calling him a flash ******* (I'm not sure what the stars stand for, but I imagine it's 'flash developer').

The headlines in the British newspapers talked about 'Roonaldo fury at Flash Beckham'. I can only imagine that will be the name of Beckham's next child, but I'm not sure why Wayne hates it so much already!

September 10 – Manchester Minor League

Yet more proof this weekend to show how bad a head coach Sir Fergie is.

Manchester had a bye week, so took on their minor league side in a practice game. You'd expect the starting roster to get the win by about five scores, yet what happens? A 1–1 tie!

It's a relief we didn't have a proper game, as Cristiano Roonaldo is missing, due to the death of his father, although his brother Wayne will still play. Maybe he didn't get on with his Dad. I know if those two were my children, Cristiano would be my favorite as well.

Rude Nistelrooy kicked the opening score deep into hurt additions at the end of the first period, continuing his incredible record of never having hit a score from any further than three yards.

Yet Joey Barton took a break from terrorizing the 16-year-old minor leaguers to grab a parallel score with 15 minutes of regulation time remaining.

And Andy Cole, a former starting offenser for Manchester before being demoted to the practice squad, almost got the win in the last second for the minors with a patriot missile of a kick, which Eddie Vandersar managed to glove behind the score-zone.

All of this shows that Sir Fergie, whose only role is to pick the best kickers, has managed to put together a roster which is slightly worse than the kickers he has ignored. He would be better off picking the team by closing his eyes and using a pin!

September 11 — Introducing the Manchester minor league side

There's little doubt that Sir Fergie is doing a terrible job as Manchester head coach, considering the kickers he has selected only tied against the kickers he thinks are rubbish.

So who are these kickers that are seemingly as good as the Manchester franchise, despite not being able to get on to the roster? Here's a guide to some of their kickingest kickers.

Joey Barton

Barton is the top kicker at the minor league side and he proved it with the parallel score against Manchester on Saturday. He is nicknamed Clinton, due to the interesting things he can do with a cigar.

Bradley 'Center' Phillips

The brother of Shaun Phillips, Bradley is a central offenser. No doubt Sir Fergie will ignore him for a long time, then trade him to the London Chelseas for a lot of money and we'll end up a further six games behind them in the EPL pennant race.

Kaspar Schmeichel

The son of the Manchester legend, who wants to follow in his Dad's footsteps by tending goal at the Nike Trafford Ballpark. He really is a french fry off the old block, being tall, blond and very, very moody. In addition, being just like his father, he also really dislikes Bradley Phillips and his entire family.

Andrew Cole

Former Manchester roster kicker, who was demoted to the minors a couple of years ago. Famous for the crowd song: 'Andy Cole, Andy Cole, Andy Andy Cole. He gets the ball, he kicks a score, but sometimes can't hit a barn door.'

Claudio Reyna

Glorious super-charged marvellous American middleman. The Glaz-meister will be furious that a top American kicker is allowed to spend his time in the minor league treatment room, rather than the main Manchester treatment room.

September 12 — Time for kickers to sort themselves out

This could be a very long series if the Manchester kickers don't sort out their attitude problem.

It's bad enough being held by our own minor league side, but now it turns out the kickers are too worried about their appearance to notice that the Glaz-meister has come to save the day.

Ryan Giggs revealed: 'We're right in the middle of it but we don't really think about it. We met in pre-season but we just said hello. The players hardly every talk about it.

They're too busy taking the pee out of each other's clothes and haircuts.'

I know Park's 'Beatles' hairstyle is about 40 years too late, but I still don't think they should be making fun of each other. I just don't think the kickers are concentrating.

I also heard that David Beckham prepared for Britain's game with Norn Iron by having a manicure. And he wasn't the only kicker to go to the beauty parlor. Ferdinand Rio had his hair puffed up for the occasion, while Wayne Roonaldo had his head washed and peeled.

September 13 — Manchester could be out of their depth

We're four games into the series and there are two franchises with four wins – the London Chelseas and the Charlton Addicts.

Kicking their home games in The Valley, Wales, the Charlton Addicts have been in the EPL for a number of years, without ever being close to the top or the bottom, until now.

So who are these little-known kickers that have vanquished EPL franchises like Sunderland and Wigan already this series? Here's a guide to their top stars.

September 14 — Introducing the Charlton Addicts

Manchester meets Real Villa in the Euro Series Wednesday night, knowing that they face a far superior franchise.

I have been rooting for Manchester for a long time now – almost five months – but they haven't had a game in the Euro Series in all that time.

I've done some research and it looks like we're coming up against some franchises that are simply much better than us. We have picked up a loss in the last three Euro Series games and haven't won a road game for two years.

It's good to test the roster against the world's top teams,

but I must warn the fans against expecting too much from these games. We are up against the very best and are clearly some way from the standard the Liverpool Reds set to win this pennant last series.

Danny Murphy

Former Liverpool Reds star, who went from Britain star to the Charlton Addicts when he found himself obsessed by bitter (which Pop says is like the beer he drinks, except warm and vile). But whatever happens to him, he never gets bitter.

Dennis Rommedahl

As fast as Carl Lewis, completing his 40-yard sprints in summer camp in 2.35 seconds. Unfortunately, he also has the skill of Carl Lewis. With the Outreach program due to his addiction to sugar.

Alexei Smertin

Rented from the London Chelseas (hence the reason they are known as the London Chelsea Rentboys). The Russian is good friends with Chelseas' GM Roman Abramovich and if he wasn't, you get the feeling he'd be playing for Metalurgs Donetsk or someone similar.

The Bent one

Still can't remember his name, but he has had a storming start to the series, kicking five scores in their opening four games. Drafted from the Ipswich Farmers, he is with the Addicts due to his fixation with the musicals of Andrew Lloyd Webber.

September 15 — Real Villa 0—0 Manchester

I have been following soccer for about five months now and I thought I knew pretty much all there is to know about the sport. But things happened yesterday that made me realize I still have a long way to go.

Wayne Roonaldo was ejected from the Euro Series clash against Real Villa for picking up two half-ejections. Kim Milton Nielsen, the first female referee in soccer, showed him a yellow piece of paper for running into an opponent. Wayne agreed with the decision and applauded her for making the correct call, yet Kim showed him the same piece of yellow paper for it and he was ejected.

Maybe the referee was upset as she made a pass at Wayne, but he turned her down as she was too young. Maybe her feet hurt. After all, she looked very tall, so probably had some very long heels on.

Everyone agreed with the decision – including Sir Fergie – yet to me it's stupid that telling the referee that she has done a good job gets you kicked off the field. It must have been the referee's time of the month.

Yet, in another game, Pop tells me that London Arsenals' African offenser Robbie Nvanpersie was ejected for kicking an opponent in the head and everyone says the referee got it wrong! How come kicking someone in the head is fine, yet congratulating the referee is bad? This game of yours is strange.

 Meanwhile, in all of this, Manchester broke their losing streak in the Euro Series with a magnificent zip-zip tie with Real Villa. Maybe we can finally stop losing all our Euro games from now on.

We were almost made to pay for the naughty ejection as Real Villa poured forward looking for the three-point score and were inches away when Marcos Senna's head-kick hit the horizontal score bar in the last minute.

September 16 — Roonaldo and his shrink

Wayne Roonaldo has been told to see a psychiatrist if he is going to fulfil his potential.

Gordon Taylor, who appears to be some kind of foster father for all EPL kickers, says that the offenser needs anger management classes if he is to avoid being given more naughty ejections and be punished by having a bath on his own.

I think that's a great idea. I imagine it would go something like this:

SHRINK: Now Wayne, tell me where your anger comes from.

WAYNE: I don't ******* know. How the **** am I meant to ******* know, you ****?

SHRINK: Now, mind your language Wayne. I was always told that if you have to swear to make your point, then you're a ****.

WAYNE: What?

SHRINK: What I meant was, calm down, calm down.

WAYNE: Ah gotcha. Well, it's just that I get so angry when things don't go my way.

SHRINK: Give me an example, Wayne.

WAYNE: Well I was furious when I was turned down for entry to the Women's Institute.

SHRINK: What did you feel then?

WAYNE: I didn't get to feel anything. That was the problem.

SHRINK: Let's concentrate on Wednesday's match. I hear Sir Fergie gave you the hairdryer treatment after the game.

WAYNE: Yeah, it was nice that he pampered me to try to make me feel better, but it didn't help.

SHRINK: How are you going to control this violent temper of yours? If you lost that, do you think you would be like Samson when he lost his hair?

WAYNE: Eh? Sir Fergie didn't cut my hair, just blow-dried it.

SHRINK: Oh, I think you misunderstood me. Let me put it in terms you might understand. Would you feel like Superman next to Kryptonite?

WAYNE: Eh? Krypton what?

SHRINK: Like Roger Redhat without his red hat?

WAYNE: Well why didn't you just say that? No, I don't think I would be. Hats don't really suit me. My head is a bit big to wear hats.

SHRINK: You mean like King Henry VIII?

WAYNE: I don't know. Most people say it's more like a King Edward.

SHRINK: Anyway, we're not here to talk about your fondness for headgear. We're here to talk about your anger.

WAYNE: I might be loaded, I don't have my own fisherman yet.

SHRINK: Oh, forget this. I support the Liverpool Reds anyway.

September 18 — Liverpool Reds 0–0 Manchester

Another great result for Machester. After finally avoiding defeat in the Euro Series in midweek, we got a second zip-zip tie on the spin against the Liverpool Reds.

It doesn't sound like it was a very good game, but we had a chance to win it, when Rude Nistelrooy put a french fry just over the 8ft horizontal bar with 1:32 remaining in the first period.

I'm so happy! I never thought Manchester was good enough to get a tie with the best team in Europe, but it really shows how far this franchise is coming on under the wonderful stewardship of Super Malcolm Glazer.

And two zip-zip ties in a row . . . we are starting to be more like the London Chelseas, who specialize in games with as few scores in as possible. They are the team with the history of success, so being like them can only be a good thing.

September 19 — Keano on the Injured Reserve

After the high of tying with the best team in Europe, comes the low for Manchester.

Roy Keano has been put on the Injured Reserve list for two months after breaking his metatarsal in the zip-zip clash with the Liverpool Reds.

Most people got their metatarsal broken four years ago. Beckham did, Gerrard did, and even Gary Neville did. Trust Keano to be late with his. Admittedly, he's late for a lot of things. Like tackles, for example.

Keano, nicknamed 'Keane' because of his love for depressing paino-led pop music, will miss Manchester's big game against the London Chelseas, as well as the clashes with the Blackburn Pyros, the Ben Fica XI and Tott Nam.

Plus, he will be unavailable for Britain's World Cup XIV divisional round games, although Sven Eriksson is such a bad head coach, he never even picks him for Team Britain anyway!

September 20 — Roonaldo the world's best child

Wayne Roonaldo has won an award for the best young kicker in the world.

The foul-mouthed (TM) Manchester star beat his brother Cristiano, London Chelseas star Arjen Robben and London Arsenals Chesc Fabregas to win the FifPro Child Kicker of the Year.

He also beat an offenser called Dong Fanzhou, who the report I read states plays for Manchester, but that's obviously not true. If he played for us, he would be in the roster instead of Rude Nistelrooy, seeing we haven't kicked a score for over 10 quarters!

Ronald Inyo of Spanish franchise the Barca Loners, won the senior award, beating Thierry Henry of the London Arsenals, Realmadrid star Zidane Zidane and Manchester's own David Bellion.

September 22 – Doncaster Osmonds 1–1 Manchester (after four halves)

Manchester have been humiliated by AA league roster the Doncaster Osmonds.

We played them in the opening round of the Carl Ing Tribute Cup – a charity pennant dedicated to the late Carl Ing, a professional kicker from the 1970s whose career was sadly ended in a freak interview accident at the age of just 21.

On the back of two zip-zip ties on the spin, Sir Fergie decided a complete change in the roster was necessary and called up all the minor league kickers for the game.

Sadly, it was another stupid decision as we were beaten yet again in a 12-yard kick-ball challenge after the game finished – yep, you guessed it – zip-zip.

That meant the teams played a further two halves to see if they could be separated. Darius Vassell, a British national franchise kicker who I expected to be involved with the first-team roster this series, kicked home a 12-yard kick-ball punishment after Richard Dunne had been hauled down in the 18-yard zone. I say 'hauled down' because it would have taken some kind of long-distance hauler to bring Dunne down.

Yet inside the two-minute warning at the end of the fourth period, Silvan Distan, a romantic Frenchman with even his name in a rhyming couplet, picked up the ball thinking the final hooter had gone and the referee again pointed to the 12-yard dot.

That proved the paralleling score and so the game went to the kick-ball challenge and we failed to kick a score in even one of the five!

The Osmonds are only in position 21 in their AA league standings and even though it was our minor league team playing, it is still embarrassing.

As if that wasn't enough proof that Sir Fergie is losing the plot, he is now refusing to talk to Manchester's Official TV network MUTV (which stands for Manchester's Uber-Truth Vehicle).

Pop says MUTV makes Soviet news agency Pravda look off-message, so who knows how they could have annoyed Sir Fergie that much. Maybe the reporter drank all the port.

September 23 — Roonaldo doll being released

Manchester are releasing a 12" doll of star offenser Wayne Roonaldo.

The Roonaldo doll has a Hand-clap action for when he is told off, a Petulant Stare feature and comes in Pottymouth and non-Pottymouth (for children under 12) versions. It is being aimed at the 50-year-old woman market.

September 24 — Manchester 1—2 Blackburn Pyros (!)

Well, that's it! Sir Fergie has completely lost the plot. And because of him, Manchester lost yet again, this time to the Blackburn Pyros.

After cutting the entire starting roster against the Doncaster Osmonds in midweek to play the minor league players, today he chose to bring back all the starters, except one – our best starter – Wayne Roonaldo. Even a garbage head coach like Sven Eriksson would know that is a stoopid thing to do.

Roonaldo was on the sidelines for the first period of the game as the Blackburn Pyros, a ferocious prison team who had travelled all the way down from the north of England, got the win.

Morten Gamst Pedersen, who is serving 10 years for defrauding his own Grandma, kicked two scores, the first an incredible kick-ball infringement, where he pretended to cross the ball, only to sneak it into the bottom corner of the score-zone.

We got back into it thanks to a clever little trick by Wayne Roonaldo. He spent the first half putting the ball under the grill, so when he came on, his shot was too hot for American Super God goaltender Brad Friedel to handle and Rude Nistelrooy grabbed another one-yard score.

But then Paul Scholes, who bravely manages to play a full role for Manchester despite the color of his hair, gave away the win. He was messing about near Eddie Vandersar's area – I think he just wanted to show all the normal-haired kickers that he was just the same as them underneath. But the Pyros' Michael Gray, who is nearing parole after serving two years for stalking a woman called Judy Finnegan, took the ball off him and Pedersen kicked another score to take the win.

Manchester have now not picked up a win for five games this series. The shouts will get louder. 'Sir Fergie out! Sir Fergie out!'

For his part, Sir Fergie released a statement, insisting that he is happily married with children.

September 25 – Introducing the Blackburn Pyros

In a move reminiscent of a bad movie starring someone like Vin Diesel or Jason Statham, the Blackburn Pyros prison franchise beat the great Manchester yesterday.

So who are the old lags that put Manchester to the sword (that's a prison euphemism, I think)? Here is my guide to the Blackburn Pyros roster.

Dominic Matteo

Drafted from Manchester's British feeder franchise, the Leeds Enrons, Matteo has the look of a man who has been in jail for too long. Currently serving time for imaginary bodily harm.

Zurab Khizanishvili

American defenseman from Georgia – somewhere near Atlanta, I think. After his performance yesterday I can't believe he hasn't kicked for Team USA yet. I'm sure he will once he serves two years for stealing all the good letters from a Scrabble board.

Craig Bellamy

It turns out just being Craig Bellamy is a criminal offense, hence the reason he is with the Pyros this series.

Paul Dickov

Aggressive short man, whose name also explains what he did to the man he caught with his wife. The first prisoner with a name describing his crime since Rodney Bankrobber.

September 26 — Sir Fergie jeered from the Ballpark

Maybe I was a bit down yesterday. Maybe things aren't so bad in Manchester after all.

So we picked up a loss on Saturday against the Blackburn Pyros, a team made up of kickers in jail for perjury or driving with undue care and attention, but it's time to look on the bright side.

For the first time in 15 years, fans at the Nike Trafford Balpark started jeering Sir Fergie, so it's great to see the new fans agreeing with veteran Manchester supporters like me.

The crowd yelled '4–4–2', which I think is Sir Phelan's internal phone number at the ballpark. Now is the time to call him before it's too late. We're already 3.5 games behind the London Chelseas and we've only played six!

I haven't seen that kind of reaction by the crowd since some of the less clever Manchester fans got the wrong end of the stick and chased a window glazer out of the Nike Trafford Ballpark.

September 28 — Manchester 2–1 Ben Fica XI

Rude Nistelrooy's late score saved Sir Fergie's job for the moment as Manchester scraped a two-to-one win over the Ben Fica XI in the Euro Series divisional round.

Ryan Giggs gave us the go-ahead score when he cleverly

aimed a 20-yard dead-kick gratis ball at a defender and got it to bounce off him into the far corner of the score-zone. Clearly, Giggs has been learning angles by playing pool in the time he has been standing on the sidelines this series.

But Fica ace Simmow bettered him in the second period, pretending he was aiming at a Manchester player in the defensive fence, but missing him and arrowing into the top section of the score net.

It was looking dodgy and the fans were starting to chant Sir Phelan's phone number again, but with five minutes left, Nistelrooy hit what was a close-range score even for him, kicking a score from less than a foot out!

But it was enough to keep Sir Fergie in his job for the moment. He reckoned it was a great win considering we were missing Keano (left foot), Neville (right groin), Heinze (knee) and Wayne Roonaldo (sarcasm).

I can't decide whether it might be worth Manchester losing a couple of games to get rid of the head coach and get someone better. Although, having said that, we play the Fulham Fayeds and Sunderland next, so it's virtually impossible that we won't get two wins from two.

I was wondering who Ben Fica is. Well, Pop tells me he never actually existed. He is one of those made-up front men, like Ronald McDonald, Tony the Tiger and David Bellion that aren't real.

September 29 — London Chelseas win the EPL

It's official! The London Chelseas have won the EPL.

Paddy Power – the head bookmaker from the Irish Mafia, the Leprechaunakuza – has paid all the people who illegally put bets on the Chelseas to win the pennant (I thought only those in Las Vegas were allowed to bet on sporting events). The spokesman, Paddy's brother Puppy, was unavailable for comment.

So that's it. I suppose the London Chelseas will parade the EPL trophy at their next hometown game against the Boltonians in two weeks. Oh well, I guess it was too much to ask that the Glazer revolution started with a pennant.

Still, second place in the standings would be better than Manchester has done for years.

September 30 — Keano to quit Manchester!

Oh no! My worst nightmare has happened. Roy Keano has announced he is going to leave Manchester at the end of the current series.

The star middleman revealed he wants to kick for another franchise and will test the free agency market over the summer. The rumors were that he would become a coach at Manchester, but understandably, he stated he had no interest in working with Sir Fergie any longer than he had to.

He is expected to go to the Glasgow-Ireland Greens to end his career. To commemorate the great man, here is a biography of Roy Keano:

Roy Keano – A Manchester Legend

Keano started his career with the Nottingham Arboretums, before being traded to Manchester in 1993.

During his time at the franchise, Keano won seven EPL pennants, four SA Super Bowls and the Euro Series, although Sir Fergie cut him from the starting roster for the Euro Series final due to his poor form and bad temper.

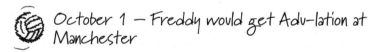 ## October 1 — Freddy would get Adu-lation at Manchester

American magno-child Freddy Adu has spoken of his desire to kick for Manchester when he grows up.

The youngster, who made his debut in Major League Soccer at the age of three, says he can't wait to join the EPL when he is old enough and he is only interested in playing for either Manchester or the London Chelseas.

I'm not really sure what to believe. He can't be that good, as

Team USA aren't great and he can't even get past Brian McBride into that roster.

Adu is the highest-paid kicker in the MLS, despite being so young that he is yet to start shaving or kiss a girl. He is being predicted to follow in the footsteps of Pelé, so he may have a problem that means he can't go any further than kissing a girl.

October 2 — Fulham Fayeds 2–3 Manchester

Manchester maintained their win-streak with a two-to-three road win at the Fulham Fayeds in an amazing game.

It's a game that will go down in history for one incredible fact – Rude Nistelrooy kicked two scores, both of which were from at least 12 yards from the score-zone!

Although having said that, one was a 12-yard kick-ball punishment and the other was a no-tender gimme-score after a great run from Park. That is amazing for him as his previous seven scores combined were only from 9 yards out!

In between, Wayne Ronaldo kicked a score after he returned to the starting roster, while Park was named the game's MVP, presumably for selling a lot of shirts on the streets outside the Cottage-Dome.

Nistelrooy's kick-scores saved Manchester, who had fallen behind on the first possession of the game, when Collins John (or John Collins . . . I can't remember which one it was) kicked the go-ahead score after two minutes. That was such a special moment for the Egyptian franchise that there will probably be a memorial to it in Harrods soon.

Manchester fought back well and took a come-from-behind lead, before Claus Jensen (or Jensen Claus . . . I can't remember again) kicked a score, identical to Ryan Giggs's last week.

But Nistelrooy had the last word, which was 'Yessss!' as he kicked the winning score.

October 3 — Rude going/Rude staying (*delete as applicable)

Rude Nistelrooy's Manchester future is in the air after his schizophrenic agent got himself all confused.

On Sunday, the Hollandish offenser's agent said that Rude wanted to be traded to Spain to play for Realmadrid, so I am assuming that he would have to commute to Portugal every day to play for them.

Then today, the agent woke all confused with a different personality and only a vague recollection of the past few days. And sure enough, he then told the reporters that he'd never said those things. He also said he had no idea how there came to be a picture of him with a stripper or where that tattoo on his butt came from.

I really hope Nistelrooy doesn't leave. Who else will kick the scores from one yard out? Wayne Roonaldo only scores them from about 25 yards, so he's no good.

I was really worried by this, so I went to a few forutne-tellers with pictures of Rude to see what they had to say about his future.

The crystal ball reader said: 'I see a stadium, with a donkey playing side by side with a cartoon monster from a film. There's a very angry man behind them and a hairdresser sitting on the sideline.'

It was at this point I told her to start looking into the crystal ball and lay off the magic mushrooms for a while.

The tarot reader said: 'You've turned over The Magician and The Fool, which shows the two sides of Rude Nistelrooy very well. But then the major arcana card is The Hermit, which indicates to me that he will be alone very soon. Maybe he's going to watch FC United play.'

The palm reader said: 'I can't read hooves.'

October 4 — Time for Glazer to expand the revolution

It's nation-on-nation shoot-out time this week, so there is a break from Manchester games for 14 days. So it's a good time to discuss how the Glazer revolution is going.

To me, things look like they are going well. Manchester are fourth in the EPL standings, 3.5 games back from the London Chelseas, but only half a game from the Charlton Addicts, the team Kate Moss supports, in second.

Ticket prices have gone up, which is great, because that means the Glaz-meister is reducing the franchise's debts, which seem quite high (lucky Super Malcolm has come in to rescue the franchise, isn't it?).

In fact, I reckon that things are going so well, that maybe Glazer and his three mini-mes should look at buying into other franchises.

Pop tells me there is another franchise close to the Nike Trafford Ballpark called FC United of Manchester. They are playing for the Moore & Co. Construction Solicitors League Division Two South pennant and are currently top of the standings. Maybe the Glaz-meister should buy them as well. It would be great to start a portfolio of franchises.

October 5 — Rio admits: 'I'm garbage'

Manchester's Ferdinand Rio has admitted he has been playing very poorly this season and it has ruined his chances of a roster spot in nation-on-nation action.

The Brazilian defenseman was jeered by Manchester rooters who thought he was greedy for refusing to share his potato chips with the other kickers and he said that has severely dented his confidence.

He was hoping to play in the Brazilian national roster this week, but is likely to be cut, where he can stand on the sidelines and not head-kick the ball, not make challenges and jump out of the way of dangerous crosses to his heart's content.

Rio is, of course, famous for forgetting how to urinate, which is a rare medical condition, suffered only by Beavis and Butthead.

October 7 — Rude back to his best

Sir Fergie is right about something! Rude Nistelrooy is back to doing what he does best. Not only is he kicking lots of scores from less than three feet, he is also getting into fights with team-mates.

After scrapping with Ferdinand Rio in a pre-series match against the Kashima Reindeers, he got into a fight with a fellow Hollandish kicker in training camp.

The Manchester soccerer was furious when Ron Vlaar kicked his kick off the score-zone line and kicked him to the ground (before attempting to steal his wallet).

Mark van Basten, who has become the Hollandish head coach despite never playing soccer himself, was livid with Nistelrooy and forced him to apologize.

'Sometimes I have a problem keeping my self-control,' said Rude, before waving at a bear that was wandering into the nearest wood with a roll of Andrex.

October 9 — Sven's superstars reach World Cup final

Team Britain are through to the World Cup final after beating Austria one-zip at the Nike Trafford Ballpark.

London Chelseas middleman Frank Lampard kicked the only score from the 12-yard kick-ball punishment dot – his first score for over a year that didn't hit a defenseman on the way in.

Defenseman Paul Scharner had come straight from the freezing climate of Austria and was still cold, so when Michael Owen touched him, he stuck to him and the referee awarded a 12-yard kick-ball punishment for freezer burn.

Former Manchester kicker David Beckham was ejected after being penalized by the referee twice in two minutes. His wife must have been furious as being sent to the locker room 30 minutes early gave him additional texting time.

The final takes place on Wednesday as Britain take on mighty Poleland, a team from the Arctic Circle, to decide what is the best soccer kicking piece of land in the world.

October 10 — Manchester casino shelved

The Las Vegas Sands Corporation has decided not to pursue their original plans to build a casino at the Nike Trafford Ballpark.

After speaking to the franchise, they have decided that the restrictions are too tight in Britain and the project isn't going to get off the ground.

I think it's a terrible shame as they were planning some great games.

Roy Keano Roulette – Which kicker will he take out next? Place your bets!

Ferdinand Rio Slot Machines – You keep putting your money in, but he keeps it all.

Wayne Poker – In which Roonaldo's friend points at a 59-year-old woman and says the name of the game.

Darren Fletcher's Craps – Not a game, just a statement.

October 13 — My trip to see Team USA

I've just had a great weekend. Because of the EPL break, Pop knew that I wouldn't have much Manchester news to write about, so surprised me with a trip to see Team USA in a nation-on-nation shoot-out.

We went to the Bruce Arena in Boston to see us get the win over Panama to finish their World Cup XIV pre-finals series with a 7-2-1 record.

The atmosphere at the Stadium was great, with all the

fans just rooting for Team USA. Manchester had Timmy Howard playing, while former defenseman Jonathan Spector was also in the starting roster.

Kyle Martino, fresh out of a sell-out run at the Bellagio hotel in Las Vegas, kicked the opening score with his first nation strike – a stunning one-timer from just beyond the left corner of the six-yard line.

Then Taylor Twellman also tallied his first strike in national play by capitalizing on a Panama defensive miscue. Seizing on a poor Panama reverse lateral, Twellman beat the onrushing goaltender to the loose ball, heading it past him and slipping the ball into the untended score-zone.

My favorite soccer chant was from the Pamana road fans who sang, to the tune of the Muppet Show: 'Panama, de de dede de. Panama, de dede de.'

It was really nice of Pop to take me to see my first soccer game, but I do have to admit I am a Britain fan now. We won our World Cup pre-final against Arctic Circle nation Poleland, finishing top of the standings.

Michael Owen grabbed a reverse sweep heel-score in the first period, before Frank Lampard's stunning one-timer with ten minutes left on the clock to beat those plucky Eskimos.

Bring on the World Cup Series, which takes place next year in Germany. I'd love the Championships game to be between Team USA and Team Britain. After we destroy Iran (in the pennant stage, obviously. Not in real life). That would be awesome!

October 14 – Jay-Z in talks with the London Arsenals

Bad news! Mega-Merican rapper Jay-Z is rumored to be in talks with the London Arsenals to buy the franchise.

It's good that more Americans are interested in soccer having seen the good work that Super Malcolm Glazer has done with Manchester. But if they get all the money that he has earned by him Keeping it Real, then they'll be harder to beat for second place in the EPL standings.

I'm not sure why it's such a surprise for everyone that Jay-Z is interested in soccer. Did they not hear his *Billboard* number one song? I've written the lyrics below to show that he's always been a London Arsenals fan.

'It's a Hard-Knock Life at the London Arsenals' Jay-Z

Take the Chelseas out, uh huh
Jigga uh huh uh huh uh huh
And we'd win the EPL.

It's second place for us (uh huh)
It's second place for us
Wayne, he dived, we get tricked
Wayne, he scores, we get kicked
It's second place!!

From taking all the corners badly
To kicking some of the hottest scores London has ever
    seen
To getting some of the dumbest cards soccer has ever
    heard
From the 12-yard kick-ball punishment spot, where the
    Sol blocked
Fleeing the ejection scene, Arsene knows he didn't see it.

From nightmares of a Manchester defeat, we got beat
But since when did Henry decide to retreat?
Where was our left corner back? Out with the Chelseas
And he wanted to leave, rubbing our noses in it and what
    not,
But we can't let him go, we must not.

Let outsiders beat our defence, and our tactics
The Middle Borough took our defence and split it 50-50,
    uh huh
Let's take the Euro Series dough and get knocked out, uh
    huh
Let's get red cards and complain, no doubt.

Flow infinitely like the memory of my captain Vieira,
    baby!

You know it was hell when we traded him
The life and times of Arsene Wenger Volume 2,

Ya'll soccer kickas get ready
It's second place for us (uh huh)
It's second place for us
Wayne, he dived, we get tricked
Wayne, he scores, we get kicked
It's second place!!

We root for those droned out
All our kickas are down and out at 10 to five after a loss
    in the house
The ref was hard, cards we don't take 'em, we take 'em
    hard
Ban 'em now and you can have Flamini back, I'd rather
    not
We live for kicks, wishing we didn't have to trade our
    captain
I see your vision mama, which is better than Arsene
    Wenger
All my kickas that born to sulk
Now we're gonna be second
Whatever I recommend
We went from hot to lukewarm.

Playing at Hi Berry on grass, the tiny size, dream kickas,
    can we score five
Fran see pies let the thing between my eyes analyze the
    Arsenals' ills
Then Lehmann puts it down, they score
They score still with the no good offensers, you might feel
    we're garbage
We're like, don't write us off,
They're still, yeah but it's two-zip
We're getting murdered by everyone. Help us!

Ya'll soccer kickas get ready
It's second place for us (uh huh)
It's second place for us
Wayne, he dived, we get tricked

Wayne, he scores, we get kicked
It's second place!!

October 15 — Sunderland 1—3 Manchester

Manchester moved up to third in the EPL standings after a three-to-one win at national side Sunderland.

Sunderland, who failed to even reach the World Cup XIV pre-finals pennant race and had to make do with a place in the EPL, were on top for much of the game, but scores from Wayne Roonaldo, Rude Nistelrooy and Giuseppe Rossi earned us the win.

Park Ji-Sung won a tackle on the half-way line, the first of his career and surged forward, finding Roonaldo, who calmly rounded goaltender Kelvin Davis and walked the ball over the score-line.

We thought we'd got the win wrapped up when Nistelrooy outpaced the defenseman – also the first time in his career – and doubled our advantage.

But you never can tell with this Manchester team. Back Sunderland came and two minutes later, they re-halved the deficit. Stephen Elliott got the score with a vicious one-timed, left-footed howitzer.

Eddie Vandersar had to make a great batted save from Anthony The Tallec's 24-yard kick-ball, but as Sunderland went on the offense, Rossi made the win safe for Manchester, belting the ball past Davis from the 25-yard line.

It's great to see Rossi, another American, on the roster for Manchester. It's clear that the influence of Super Malcolm Glazer is making Manchester a better franchise.

Obviously, the London Chelseas are still a mile clear. They kicked five scores in a second period in a zero-to-three-point turnaround against the Boltonians, the posh team from a boarding school, who must have been regretting staying up all night putting Ricardo Gardner's hand in warm water while he slept.

But we moved a game ahead of the London Arsenals after

their shock loss to the Western Bromwiches. N. 'Wankwo' Kanu silenced his critics by kicking a score, having previously played for the Arsenals.

October 16 — Paul Scholes: A correction

I have been reading through the player profiles I wrote when I started following Manchester and I think I may have made a mistake.

I wrote that Paul Scholes was one of the top scoring middlemen in the EPL, but it turns out I was wrong. His score-kicking record is terrible and he hasn't found the scoring zone in the last 23 games.

It turns out he is more of an anchor man, which is a soccer slang term meaning he is getting on a bit and doesn't run around as much as he used to, so it looks like he has an anchor tied to his leg.

In addition, he is not getting picked for the Britain team either, so he is another kicker that Sir Fergie rates highly, but Sven Eriksson, the nation's top head coach, thinks is less good that Owen Hargreaves – and that's strong criticism.

There is one thing that Scholes is still one of the best in the business at though and that is tackling opponents so late that they are boarding the bus on the way home. I'm sure he'll show his speciality against the Lille Savages on Tuesday, a team filled with people who grew up on a desert island following a plane crash.

They have a few injury problems though. Jack Bodmer and Ralph Tavlaridis are expected to be fit, but Piggy will have to make do with a place on the bench.

October 17 — Could Sir Fergie be leaving Manchester?

Good news Buccs fans! Sir Fergie is considering leaving Manchester to take over as head coach of nation franchise Ireland.

Former Manchester corner-defenseman Denis Irwin revealed that his best friend's cousin's mistress's mailman is fairly sure he saw Sir Fergie going into a restaurant which some Irish people sometimes go into. So there seems a great deal of truth in this.

It seems a strange choice for Sir Fergie, as Ireland don't even enter the World Cup Series pre-finals round – featuring in that competition as a part of Team Britain. But without a pennant victory in quite some time, perhaps head coaching a sub-regional roster is his level.

The current head coach of Ireland is Brian Kerr, but he is expected to leave to coach in Spain, where he will be known by his nickname of 'Juan'.

October 18 — Roonaldo still out for Manchester

Manchester returns to Euro Series action today as we take on the Lille Savages.

We are currently leading the standings in the race for a Euro pennant and must surely be confident of getting a win against the French franchise, especially after beating a whole country on Saturday with the win over Sunderland.

Not that we will have all our starters available. Alan Smith is questionable, while Roy Keano (foot), Gary Neville (groin) and Wayne Roonaldo (the clap-hand variety) are all definitely on the Injured Reserve.

October 19 — Manchester 0–0 Lille Savages

Manchester were held to a zip-zip tie by French franchise the Lille Savages in the latest Euro Series match.

Without Wayne Roonaldo, who was taking a well-earned romantic break at the Women's Institute, we struggled to find a way through the Lille defensemen, who blitzed Rude Nistelrooy throughout.

Ryan Giggs hit the vertical bar with a kick-ball punishment from the 25-yard line, but that was the closest we came to breaking the zip-lock (although somehow Wayne managed to break his zipper last night).

Giggs picked up a broken jaw during the game, which means that our Injured Reserve list is now so long that Sir Fergie has had to go on to the second side of the A4 paper.

But it's not all bad news. Like I said, after a slow start to this series, Paul Scholes is back to doing what he does best – clattering into opponents long after the ball is gone and being ejected. You never lose that kind of skill.

October 20 — Shock news! Roonaldo arrested

Manchester star Cristiano Roonaldo has been arrested on suspicion of rap.

According to the British Broadcasting Company, the arrest is part of an investigation into allegations of an indecent rap at a hotel in central London on October 2. He must have been singing that Jay-Z song about the London Arsenals because that is pretty indecent.

I asked Pop what all of this meant and he told me that he must have sworn at a lady in rhyming couplets, which is enough to be picked up by the police in somewhere as polite as England.

Roonaldo is one of Manchester's star kickers and it would be a disaster to lose him, either to jail or to a record company. He has one score in 15 games this season and a step-over-to-centre ratio of 37.6, which is the highest in the EPL by 35.

October 21 — Iron Mike — the new Manchester head coach?

I think I've discovered who the new head coach of Manchester should be. Step forward boxer Mike Tyson.

The former world heavyweight champion wants to sit down with Wayne Roonaldo and sort out his behaviour on the soccer field.

Iron Mike told the London *Times*: 'I'd like to meet Wayne Roonaldo. I've been watching him and Manchester recently and he's been having some trouble with his behavior on the pitch. I could relate to what he was going through.'

It's not just Wayne Roonaldo that he would be able to help. He would definitely be able to give some guidance to Cristiano Roonaldo after this week's problems, as he is a convicted rapper. Who can forget his *Billboard* top 10 hit 'You can't punch this'?

And being the self-styled 'baddest man on the planet', he'd even be able to teach Roy Keano a thing or two. The only thing he would lack is a decent knowledge of hairdressing to be able to dry the players' hair if they are struggling at the half-time show.

October 22 — Rio desperate to get back in action

Ferdinand Rio showed up his team-mates by showing up for work even when he has the day off, proving just how much he wants to kick for Manchester.

The Brazilian defenseman, an extremely generous soul who kindly dropped his wage demands by 35,000 English dollars a week, was so desperate to get back to EPL action that he turned up for work on Wednesday, despite having kicked in the game the night before.

While he was there, he gave reporters a fascinating insight into the hectic lifestyle that makes him quite so forgetful. He said, 'In the morning I always have Coco Pops for my breakfast with bananas and then strawberry yogurt. Then I go into training where I always have my left ankle strapped to make sure I don't injure it. It's just something I always do. When I get home in the afternoon I just like to watch TV. I watch that program *Loose Women* and sometimes *Trisha*. I just watch whatever's on.'

I've done some research and it turns out not to be a program from the Fantasy Channel, but is actually a chat show featuring vaguely famous women who have nothing better to do than sit around in a studio and drink cheap wine. A review of the program that Mister Internet showed me said that 'you'd have to be high to enjoy this.'

October 23 — Manchester 1—1 Tott Nam

Manchester fell another game behind the London Chelseas after being held to a one-each tie by Tott Nam.

The biggest battle of the game was in midfield where the psychotic Alan Smith went toe-to-toe with the even more psychotic Edgar Davids. I think it would have ended in a fight in the car park, but Smith knows you can't hit a man in glasses.

Michael Silvester broke the zip-zip tie just six minutes after the opening buzzer with a classic Nistelrooy score (meaning it was from two yards or less).

It came as Britain goaltender Paul Robinson, who was still jetlagged after the long flight from Ramsey Street, blocked a Nistelrooy head-kick, but FUMBLE! And Silvester slid in to make it one-zip.

But Tott Nam came back into the game when young Vietnamese kid Jermaine Jenas kicked a 27-yard field kick-ball attempt into the top corner of the score-zone.

So the Tott Nam fans were thrilled, staying ahead of

Manchester in the standings as they started their long trip back to Ho Chi Minh City. Now even rugby team the Wigan Warriors are above us. Although that seems unfair as they do get three points for every score.

In other action, the London Arsenals edged past our minor league side one-zip, although I understand it was so easy that they spent the entire second period doing trick plays.

One score up, they were awarded a 12-yard kick-ball punishment when Stephen Jordan sent Denis Bergkamp flying, the highest the Dutchman has been since 1994. Robert Pires, who scored an earlier 12-yard kick-ball punishment, ran up to the ball and instead of shooting, tried to make a lateral pass to Thierry Henry, but scuffed his kick and one of our defensemen cleared.

It's alarming that the London Arsenals are winning games so easily they can afford to mess around. You'd certainly never see Rude Nistelrooy trying to pass from a 12-yard kick-ball punishment. Although to be honest, I don't think you'd ever see Rude pass, period.

October 24 — Happy birthday Wayne!

Happy Birthday Wayne Roonaldo! Manchester's star player celebrates his 20th birthday today.

The Britain star leaves his teenage years (which I am soon to enter) behind him, which means that he is no longer allowed to throw tantrums, drink alcoholic cider or split up with girls with a text message saying 'i + u = bad. c ya, innit'.

His birthday wish list was leaked on the internet, so here is what Britain's top soccer wanted for his birthday:

1) A bike. One of those really cool ones where my mate can stand behind me as I ride it wickedly fast down a hill.
2) A fireman's helmet.
3) An Everton Stickies duvet cover, single sized because I'm not sharing it with Colleen.
4) A subscription to *Saga* magazine.
5) A lot of pies.

Wayne is celebrating by moving into a new custom-built house with his girlfriend/personal shopper Colleen. It looks like a well cool house. There is a swimming pool, cinema and soccer field, while it has a separate wing containing a retirement home for females.

At the bottom of the pool, there is a mosaic with the couple's initials – WC – which could be a problem if Wayne gets really drunk and thinks he'd found the bathroom.

October 25 – Soccer Association are kind to Manchester

The Soccer Association (SA) have admitted they feel sorry for Manchester and have let them back into the Carl Ing Tribute

We were humiliated in the last round of the pennant by the Doncaster Osmonds, when Sir Fergie chose to name a starting roster consisting entirely of our minor league side to give the top kickers a break.

Yet, due to our poor recent form, the SA has allowed Manchester back into the competition in the next round! We are due to kick against the Barnet Hairdressers Wednesday.

And has Sir Fergie learnt his lesson? No. He is going to cut the entire starting roster yet again. I know we have been kicking badly recently, but cutting the Roonaldo brothers is crazy! Instead, 'stars' like Gerard Pique, Lee Martin and Sylvain Ebanks-Blake are expected to play.

That's why we need to get rid of Sir Fergie. You'd never see one of the top head coaches in the world like Arsene Wenger do that in this pennant.

October 26 – Ask Roswell – Part 2

Not much going on with Manchester today, so I thought I'd answer some more of your e-mails.

CHAY: You've gotta see this . . . Manchester biscuits!! They cost less than a pound. I predict that the marketing people will be sacked soon. Why? Rude Nistelrooy on the packet . . . that only cuts the sale.

ROSWELL: It's great to see the innovative Super Malcolm Glazer coming up with new ways of making money. But I heard that the Manchester cookies often have a bitter taste and fall apart too easily.

BRADFORDCITYTILLIDIE: When will we get another opportunity to 'Ask Ros'?

ROSWELL: Now seems like a good time. Are you glad you asked? By the way, why are you called Bradfordcitytillidie? Who are Bradford City? I know there's a minor league team called the Bradford T'Bantams (hence the reason you always hear the shout 'Come on t'Bantams'). Are the franchises related?

BENSIMPSON3: you don't no nothing about man utd i tink u shud take da manchester buccaneers down right away coz glazer is scum.if u knew netin bout football u will knw that man utd had diego forlan n den sold him 2 villereal u dick feature, football is not an americanized sport so dnt put goal tender etc dats hockey m8, n head kick its overhead i tink u shud learn the terminology first m8 n den support utd.

ROSWELL: Thank you for your message. I've been having some English lessons, so let me see if I can translate this for you.

'You do not know nothing (meaning I know lots) about Manchester – we're united in that. I think you should take down some notes about the Manchester Buccaneers right away because Glazer talks really quickly.

'If you knew netting, you'd know about soccer. You will know that Manchester had the chance to draft Diego Forlan, but locked him out of the den and he went to Real Villa instead. Soccer is not a sport that's big in America, so don't put your goaltender in front of ones from other countries.

'I'm dating a hockey player, my little eight-ball. I'm

110

head-kick over heels-kick in love with him. I think you should learn the terminology of love, then we can be truly united.'

October 27 – Manchester 4–1 Barnet Hairdressers

Manchester achieved a four to one win against the Barnet Hairdressers to move into the 1/8 final of the Carl Ing Cup pennant.

However, it might have been different if we didn't have any help. The Soccer Association are still feeling sorry for our poor run of form, so told the referee to make sure we got the win. Thank Bush he did, as the first 100 seconds were a really tight affair.

Then in the second minute, the Hairdressers goaltender was sent for an early cut and blow-dry when he touched the ball with his hands half an inch outside the handling zone. Barnet had to remove their star score-kicker, as he had an appointment to do a blonde highlights job on a 53-year-old woman, and the back-up tender came in.

The first thing he had to do was pick the ball out the score-zone after Liam Miller's 20-yard curling kick-ball. Actually, that was the second thing, as the first thing was to rub his eyes to check that Liam Miller still played for Manchester.

Britain star Keiron Richardson added a second, kicking a Ryan Giggs score – curling a wide dead-kick past everyone and into the far corner of the score-zone.

Super Giuseppe Rossi, who is as American as invading a Middle Eastern country, made it three, firing home from Lee Martin's cut back. Rossi is starting to look like an EPL-class offenser, becoming as clinical as a prostate exam.

A Hairdressers kicker did get a score, as his effort deflected off one of those huge hairdryer machines past Timmy Howard, but 13-year-old Sylvain Ebanks-Blake notched his first score to make the win safe.

It was sad Martin did not finish the game after spotting a pretty girl in the crowd and not paying attention to where he was running, crashing into the advertising hoardings. Manchester drafted him from the MK Wimbledons for one million English dollars – a million more than Beckham, Giggs and Scholes combined. He's bound to be great!

But the game was notable for the lowest crowd at the Nike Trafford Ballpark for six years. It's good to see Manchester fans voting with their feet and insisting they will not watch the Buccaneers until Sir Fergie leaves his head coach position.

If we're not careful and don't improve pretty quickly, Nike will take away their sponsorship of the stadium. After all, the marketing director of Nike said this week: 'Chelsea won the league this year, Arsenal won the FA Cup and Liverpool won the Champions League. You could argue that Manchester United is only the fourth-best club in England right now.'

October 28 – Win the next two, or that's it!

Eddie Vandersar says Manchester's series will be over if we don't win our next two games.

We travel the short distance to the Middle Borough tomorrow and Paris, France for Wednesday's Euro Series clash with the Lille Savages. As if that's not bad enough, after that comes the game against the unbeaten London Chelseas.

But the Hollandish goaltender has warned that anything less than two victories in those games will make the encounter with the EPL champion franchise virtually meaningless and we may as well spend the rest of the series picking up rubbish on the freeway.

He said: 'The season is going to stand or fall on our two results this week. There is already a gap between ourselves and Chelsea, so that will only be an important game if we win tomorrow.'

Luckily, there is no chance at all of us losing to the Lille

Savages and I'd be surprised if we picked up a loss at the Middle Borough.

October 29 — The Middle Borough 4–1 Manchester

Well I can't say I'm surprised. I have been a Manchester fan for a long, long time and everyone knows that I know that Sir Fergie is garbage. At last, other people are catching up with me.

Manchester were handed a record loss Saturday by local rivals the Middle Borough, from the inner-city projects in London, as we were demolished four to one.

Having only ever lost by one score in the history of the EPL, we were hammered by a team whose offenser Jimmy 'Floyd' Hasselbank is 53 years old. (Hasselbank's nickname is Floyd because he looks like he ran into The Wall).

I would go into more detail – how Eddie Vandersar dropped a ball into the score-zone, or how Keiron Richardson tried to pull a Borough player and conceded a 12-yard kick-ball punishment – but I'm too depressed. To lose by three scores is bad enough, but to lose a London derby is just too much.

The only bright point was Cristiano Roonaldo's head-kick score with seconds left on the clock – a goal that will for ever be featured in the dictionary next to the word *consolation*.

We kick against the London Chelseas next Sunday, already four games behind them and it looks like Wayne Roonaldo couldn't score in a Women's Institute meeting. I only pray we don't lose by five scores.

October 30 — Rossi's Rude awakening

I didn't think it could get any worse than yesterday, but the bad news keeps on piling up for Manchester this week.

Giuseppe Rossi, America's brightest prospect after Kirsten

Dunst, is Manchester's top college kicker and is expected to be one of our top offensers in the future.

You'd hope that he would get expert training and advice, yet Rossi has revealed that he has learnt everything he knows so far from Rude Nistelrooy.

Rude's a top offenser, but wouldn't it be better to pick a better role-model? Because of 'The Van', so far Rossi's specialities are arching his back as he throws himself to the floor, having really bad hair and limping.

Meanwhile, Sir Fergie has insisted that Manchester is one of the biggest franchises there is. He said: 'We are the biggest ever on the planet, in the universe. No doubt about that,' completely forgetting about the Uranus Klingons, who constantly come top of the biggest franchise in the Biggest Soccer Franchise polls.

October 31 — Happy Hallowe'en!

I'd been looking forward to today for ages. Me and my buddies Chuck, Chip and Charlie have been planning our trick or treating for ages. Not even Saturday's embarrassing defeat could ruin this night.

Chuck painted his face bright yellow and went in baseball gear, saying he was Homer Simpson. For some reason, when he approached our neighbors' front door, with a baseball bat, they gave us lots and lots of candy.

Chip had a huge stomach, big ears and ridiculous red hair. I wish he had decided to wear a costume.

I died my hair bright orange and gave it a big perm. That's right, I went as Wes Brown!

People kept asking me if I was meant to be Napoleon Dynamite. I asked who he was and they said he was a cult. I told them Pop calls Wes Brown something similar.

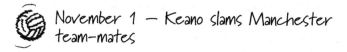

November 1 – Keano slams Manchester team-mates

I've been a Manchester fan for ages and Roy Keano has always been my favorite kicker. After what he said today, I only like him more!

Keano ripped into part of the franchise's roster, claiming that they are not good enough at kicking to play for Manchester. It's not entirely surprising he said this though. Let's not forget this is the man who admitted deliberately hurting a team-mate – a member of Manchester's minor league side – during an exhibition game.

His comments have been criticized and the interview was cut from the Official TV station MUTV. But have a look at who he criticizes and I defy you to argue with him.

Alan Smith

This is the kicker that is supposed to replace Keano in the 'holding' middleman position. The only things he has in common with the great man are a 50-year-old's name and a love of knee-high tackles.

Jono Shea

Pop says Shea burst on to the scene three years ago and looked like Denis Irwin. He still looks like Irwin now, but unfortunately, Irwin is 40.

Keiron Richardson

Keano reckons Richardson should have been traded to the Western Bromwiches when we had the chance and this is the one thing I don't agree with him on. Richardson played brilliantly for Britain as they beat Team USA. It's just that the useless Sir Fergie is playing him as a defenseman, whereas a popular coach like Sven Eriksson lists him as an offensive middleman.

Liam Miller

Remind me which one he is again.

Darren Fletcher

Sir Fergie loves him, constantly going on about how
Fletcher is going to lead the new Manchester Empire. I can
only assume it means he is going to be the manager of a
concert venue.

So it looks like Keano is only saying what long-term fans
like me know and Sir Fergie doesn't. Let's get the dream
team of Keano and Sir Phelan to replace our ageing
hairdresser head coach.

November 2 — Rio: Should he stay or should he go?

More details are coming out about the Roy Keano interview.
On top of laying into the younger kickers on the roster, he
saved some bile for Ferdinand Rio.

The Brazilian defenseman has been made the scapegoat
for the loss to the Middle Borough, with Keano saying: 'Just
because you are paid £120,000-a-week and play well for 20
minutes against Tottenham, you think you are a superstar.

'It seems to be in this club that you have to play badly to
be rewarded. Maybe that is what I should do when I come
back. Play badly.' That explains Paul Scholes's recent form, I
suppose.

So is Ferdinand Rio worth the trouble? Should Manchester
keep him or trade him? I've weighed up his pros and cons.

Pro – Pop says he sometimes reminds him of Bobby Moore.
Con – As Bobby Moore is now, I assume.

Pro – He's one of our most experienced kickers.
Con – He's so forgetful, he doesn't remember any of those
experiences.

116

Pro – He gives the franchise a Brazilian touch.

Con – Roy Keano doesn't need someone to do his bikini line.

November 3 — Lille Savages 1—0 Manchester

Crisis franchise Manchester (TM) has stumbled to yet another loss, this time to the Lille Savages in the Euro Series divisional stage.

Milenko Acimovic kicked the only score of the game when he found a gap in the Manchester defense that you could drive a stretch-Hummer through and hammered the soccer ball into the top corner of the score-zone.

Cristiano Roonaldo almost got the paralleling-score when he had a free head-kick, but he miscued it, it hit his arm, then the horizontal post, before bouncing out again. The loss leaves Manchester with just one win from four games and, at this rate, we face missing out on the Euro Series play-offs.

After the game, Rude Nistelrooy said; 'We had difficulty finding each other.' Now I realize what the problem is! Pop tells me that a few years ago, Manchester lost to the South Hamptons because they were wearing grey jerseys that they couldn't see.

I really don't know what is wrong with Manchester at the moment, or what can be done to put it right. A lot of people are saying we need a kicker like Phil Neville back in the squad, but I don't think we've sunk that far quite yet.

November 4 — The Manchester movie theater

Sir Fergie has forced all the Manchester kickers to sit through the infamous Roy Keano interview in the aftermath of the defeat to the Lille Savages.

The screening was a punishment for another poor display and, because Darren Fletcher was caught sniggering at the back, they were then made to watch it again, this time with an interpreter so they could actually understand it.

It turns out that this wasn't the first time Roy Keano had criticized his team-mates. Apparently, there is another tape hidden in the Nike Trafford Ballpark where Keano lays into Ole Solskjaer – presumably wondering whether the offenser is actually a figment of people's imagination.

And in a third tape, Keano, in full ranting mode, blamed the state of the world on little fluffy bunnies, before going on to tell children that Santa Claus, the Tooth Fairy and Liam Miller don't exist.

November 5 – Rude awakening for Paddy Vieira

Irish international Paddy Vieira has revealed his hatred for Rude Nistelrooy.

In his book about his life, from growing up a small boy in Donegal to becoming one of the world's top soccer kickers, entitled From The Coors to The Scores, he calls Nistelrooy a cheat and a coward.

He also calls him a son of a bitch, which is unfair as he is actually a son of a mare.

According to Pop, Vieira's rows with the Manchester offenser started when he got a naughty ejection for pretending to kick Nistelrooy. Unfortunately Rude overestimated the length of Vieira's legs, believing them to be nine feet long, when in actual fact they were only seven. Rude threw himself away from the flailing limb and, thinking he had received a fatal blow, the referee, a farmer in his spare time, ejected Vieira and told him to get off his land.

Manchester have been trying to draft kickers known as 'the new Vieira' for years and there were even reports that they were going to move for the old one when the trade door is unlocked in January. But I can't believe he is going to join us with Rude still on the roster. Unless, I suppose, he joins us Donnie Brasco-style and takes Rude down from the inside.

Manchester v London Chelseas preview

It's our biggest game of the series so far and it couldn't come at a worse time as Manchester find themselves in demotion form, currently sitting in a two-game losing streak.

So what chance do we have of picking up a win against the EPL champion franchise? I have done a head-to-head on the rosters to see how they compare.

John Terry v Wayne Roonaldo

The best offenser against the best defenseman, this is going to be a brilliant battle. Roonaldo has been in fine form recently, despite our dire form, and he loves big games. John Terry is like Dr Magnetron, a super hero who attracts soccer balls like magnets attract metal.

Frank Lampard v Darren Fletcher

Erm . . . well, there's definitely only one game-winner out of these two. And it's not going to be the lanky one in red.

Ferdinand Rio v Didier Drogba

I wonder which Ferdinand Rio turns up, the good one or the garbage one? Pop says Rio is like a mixture of some British TV presenter brothers called Jonathan and Paul Ross. On form, he is Jonathan – the all-conquering one who is the best in the business. Currently, he's more like Paul – the balding, chubby annoying one who presents terrible daytime shows on cable channel 183 to pay his alimony. Drogba is a battering ram, who is almost as good at head-kicking as Peter Crouch.

Peter Czech v Eddie Vandersar

These two goaltenders will be 100 yards away, so I'm not sure why people put them 'head to head'. But if I have to, I would say that Eddie Vandersar has excelled this series, making Manchester more secure in the D. Peter Czech from the Czech Republic is behind the world-best London Chelseas defense, so he is yet to see the soccer ball this series.

Sir Fergie v Jose Mourinho

No contest here. One is the Special One. One will be sacked soon and serving Special number one in his local Little Chef. I think we all know who the more successful head coach here is.

So that's how the teams square up off the pitch and the London Chelseas have a clear advantage. I just pray that their advantage on the field isn't too great as well.

November 6 — Manchester 1–0 London Chelseas

Go Buccs! Wooooooooooo!
  Manchester consigned the EPL champions London Chelseas to their first loss in 40 games, a run stretching back to 1983.
  Darren Fletcher, a kicker I've always thought was brilliant (as does Roy Keano), got the only score with a one-time cross-head-kick that looped high into the air and snuck into the corner of the netting.
  The London Chelseas controlled the possession ratio in the second half, but rarely looked like finding a parallel score. Their only two real red-zone offenses came as Eddie Vandersar blocked well at Frank Lampard's feet and Damien Duff was free on the six-yard line, but hit an O2 kick.
  With Herman Crespo in a mood, Didier Drogba was the sole offenser for the Chelseas and nothing stuck to him all game. Except his hair, that is.

Crisis franchise London Chelseas (TM) are now on a two-game losing streak and have only picked up one win in their last five games. They must be terrified, looking over their shoulder to see the Wigan Warriors, currently the best franchise in Britain, coming up fast behind them!

Meanwhile, Manchester are back! Third position at the end of the series could yet be ours! I have officially repicked up my towel, having thrown it in after the Middle Borough defeat.

After all, the last time we won a pennant in 1999, the London Chelseas hadn't even been invented yet!

Eddie Vandersar, meanwhile, didn't celebrate this win as the game was virtually meaningless in his eyes.

November 7 – Wenger and Mourinho join me in the school playground

The two head coaches of Manchester's two biggest rivals – after the Wigan Warriors – have been involved in a furious argument this week.

- Mourinho called Wenger a 'voyeur' for talking more about the London Chelseas than his own team.
- Wenger called Mourinho stupid.
- Mourinho said he had compiled a 120-page dossier of Wenger talking about the London Chelseas.
- Wenger said Mourinho must have too much time on his hands.
- Mourinho said Wenger was jealous of the London Chelseas' success.
- Wenger said, 'I know you are but what am I?'
- Mourinho said, 'Yeah, well you smell.'
- Wenger said, 'My Dad's bigger than your Dad.'
- Mourinho called Wenger 'four-eyes'.
- Wenger said Mourinho reminded him of a Mediterranean waiter who gets together with British girls while they're on vacation and gives them a disease.

- Mourinho said he had compiled a 120-page dossier, stating that Wenger had weapons of mass destruction hidden in the Marble Halls at Hi Berry.
- Wenger said Mourinho was part of the Axis of Evil.
- Mourinho said he'd say sorry if Wenger said sorry at the same time.
- Wenger said he'd only say sorry if Mourinho gave him back his Buckaroo.

I can't wait to find out what happens next!

November 8 – Sir Phelan gets a promotion!

I think Sir Fergie is reading this website.

Sadly, that doesn't mean he's resigned, but it does mean that he has promoted Sir Michael Phelan to replace Carlos Quieroz as sideline coordinator!

Sir Fergie has gagged Quieroz, stopping him shouting instructions on the sidelines. Presumably as the kickers couldn't work out whether he was telling them to play 'two banks of four' or 'Tube Ranks of War', which is a popular strategic board game in the US, where each player owns a Subway line and has to try to destroy the others without harming his own.

Ferdinand Rio, meanwhile, thought he had been saying 'Two bags of flour' which explains why he's been playing like he is carrying two bags of flour for the last few months.

Portugalese Quieroz, who had a short spell in charge of his hometown club Realmadrid, has been getting more and more unpopular with both the players and the fans at the Nike Trafford Ballpark.

The fans have shown their dislike of him by shouting 'Attack, attack', a clear reference to when Britain invaded Portugal in 1991 when they refused to side with them on the Gulf War.

Still, at last everyone is happy and Manchester's winningest coach gets a chance to show that he has the potential to replace Sir Fergie. This is turning into a great week.

November 9 — Liverpool Reds are getting cheesy

Oh no, the Liverpool Reds could be the new London Chelseas. The Euro Series champion is in talks with American billionaire Robert Kraft, the richest man in Vermont.

Kraft currently owns the three-time NFL champion New England Patriots and the top MLS soccer side the New England Revolution. I'm scared that he'll turn the Liverpool Reds into the third champion team he owns.

Kraft, who made his money selling processed cheese slices, is keen to either buy a substantial share of the 12th best team in the EPL or to buy the naming rights for Ann's Field. I believe he wants to call it Edamfield.

He is also taking a look at the kickers' image rights and I've heard that he is keen to change the name of some of the Reds' top stars. They'll have Jon Arne Brie-se and head coach Rafeta Benitez. He'll also try to trade for more kickers from Argentina.

If he takes over, Kraft also wants to try a number of new initiatives to get more fans to watch the Liverpool Reds. He wants to introduce new chants to the crowd, changing the franchise song to be 'You'll Never Walk Provalone', while he would want fans to start singing 'Camembert you Reds'.

November 10 — Roy? Sir Fergie says Kea-no

Sir Fergie is sinking to a new low – sabotaging his own kickers!

Roy Keano is regularly tipped to succeed Sir Fergie, but the under-fire Manchester head coach has told him there's no chance of that happening.

Sir Fergie said that young managers find it very hard and

rarely work out for a franchise. He then went on to say that they also end up just drafting their buddies and they all have cooties.

I think it's Sir Fergie covering his own back and trying to get rid of the competition for his own job. He knows that the fans have turned against him and want Keano and Sir Phelan to replace him.

November 11 — Introducing the Wigan Warriors

With crisis franchise London Chelseas suffering a major drop in form, it is the Wigan Warriors that are officially the top franchise in Britain right now.

They are second in the standings, two games clear of Manchester, and are currently on a win-streak of eight games. Yet before the series started, everyone marked them down for certain demotion (except me. I always thought they would do well).

So who are these new star kickers, who come from the north of Britain and talk as if they are in a Wallace and Gromit film? Here's a guide to their top men.

Pascal Chimbonda

The star of the show so far for the Warriors, he has head-kicked point-getting scores in the last two games, despite starting at cornerback. That's a remarkable return from a kicker drafted from Bastia, a team filled with players from a French orphanage and workhouse.

Jason Roberts

Transferred from the Wigan Warriors' sister team, which plays a sport called rugby (it's a bit like our football, but with more mud and less hip-hop dance celebrating). Roberts has the build of a rugby player, meaning he is huge and has ugly ears.

Henry Camara

The brother of TV soccer analyst Chris, everything Henry does is unbelievable. Normally, that's because you simply can't believe that he has aimed at the score-zone from the 40-yard line, when with a simple lateral, a team-mate could have been man-on-man with the goaltender.

Stephane Henchoz

The Swiss defenseman was a member of the Euro Series-winning Liverpool Reds roster last year, but the Wigan Warriors persuaded him to join them. When a kicker with this quality becomes available, Manchester should be after him, but the fact that the Warriors beat us to it shows our position in the EPL hierarchy.

A little-known fact about the franchise is that The Warriors don't play in Wigan, but actually play in a small town on the outskirts called Leighton Baines.

 ## Who wants some nation-on-nation action?

All Manchester's kickers are back in nation-on-nation action this weekend.

Britain travel to the Argentinia city of Geneva to take on their old enemies to play for the Faulklands Cup.

Peter Crouch will be cut, with Wayne Roonaldo and Michael Owen as the offensers. Ledley King will continue to play in the anchor position, with David Beckham on port and Joe Cole on starboard on the good ship Britain.

But Britain will be without any of their Scottish stars – on the off-chance that any of them would be selected – as Scotland are hosting Team USA.

Top US striker Brian McBride will miss the game with a tightening of his groin and as I'm approaching my teenage years, I know all about that little problem.

I said 'all Manchester's kickers', but obviously Roy Keano

has been ignored by Sven Eriksson yet again, while Rude Nistelrooy has withdrawn from the Hollandish roster after receiving a ribbing from team-mates. I think it was over his schoolboy hairstyle, but I'm not sure.

November 12 — Manchester's locker room bugged

Manchester's locker room was bugged during the 'virtually meaningless' (Copyright E. Vandesar) clash with the London Chelseas.

In a move reminiscent of the KGB, Sir Fergie's talks before, during the half-time show and after the final hooter were all recorded and offered to British newspaper the London *Sun*.

They refused to say exactly what happened, but I managed to find a full transcript of the speech:

SIR FERGIE: We're doing well. We're in a good si-u-asssshion.

But you've got to stop giving away so many kick-balls and when you punt the ball long, keep it away from John Terry. And most importantly, and I can't stress this enough, keep the ball away from Darren Fletcher. I know the lad scored, but our best chance of a win is to make sure he doesn't touch the ball again.

Now Rude, for you, it's the opposite. I would like you to touch the ball at least once this half. Do you think you can manage it?'

RUDE NISTELROOY: Yes, Sir. Of course, Sir. Right away, Sir.

SIR FERGIE: Good boy. Have a carrot. Now, Smithy . . . you're our holding man in the middle, so we need you to take responsibility for Frank Lampard.

ALAN SMITH: I'll try, gaffer, but he's t'better man than me.

SIR FERGIE: OK, well if you can't take responsibility, at least try to take him out, knee-high.

ALAN SMITH: You mean play to my strengths?

SIR FERGIE: Exactly. Now go out there boys and let's show the Chelseas that they're not the only franchise that can bore others into submission. I want you to start holding the ball in the corners as much as possible for the last 35 minutes. Now, all hands in . . . what do we say? Three, two, one.

ALL: Luck!

SIR FERGIE: Go on lads, we might get lucky!

After the game, the kickers returned to the locker room and were jubilant!

FERDINAND RIO: Jose Mourinho, Roman Abramovich, Ken Bates, John Major, Tim Lovejoy. Your boys took one hell of beating. Tell me I'm rubbish now. Tell me!

ROY KEANO: Don't tempt me, Rio. Don't tempt me.

EDDIE VANDERSAR: Why are you so happy? So we only come seven wins behind the London Chelseas instead of eight. So what? Do you ever wonder what the point of it all is?

FERDINAND RIO: Well, I can see you're going to lie face down in a darkened room tonight. What's everyone else up to? I'm off to that trendy bar that's just opened – Walkabout.

ROY KEANO: I'm going to tell my five-year-old son how bad he was as a tree in his school play. He just wasn't believable at all! I mean, what kind of tree waves at its Mummy?

WES BROWN: Wow, that's spooky. Tonight, I'm performing in a Alderton Edge Village Hall version of *Hair*.

WAYNE ROONALDO: I'm going to watch *Calendar Girls* on DVD alone again.

November 13 — Britain wins, Team USA humiliated

Michael Owen head-kicked two scores in the last five minutes as Britain achieved a double come-from-behind win over the Argentinias to win the Faulklands Cup in Geneva.

The tall Newcastle offenser easily outjumped the Argentinia defensemen to earn Britain's first pennant since

World Cup VIII 40 years ago.

The win is proof that Britain can win the World Cup next year, having failed to even qualify for the tournament since 2002. British fans are so confident that they won't lose to Argentinia again, that they even sang: 'You'll never have the Faulklands [Cup].' It's impressive that so many fans travelled all the way to Argentinia for the game anyway!

Before the game, the atmosphere in Geneva was marred

 when the Argentinian roster sang anti-British songs, calling all the kickers 'fags'. There's no room in soccer for that kind of thing. I happen to know for a fact that that isn't true for at least two of the British team.

Owen's goals, inside the five-minute warning, followed a pulsating game where London Chelseas star Herman Crespo had given his nation the lead. Wayne Bridge, who looked so far out of his depth that David Hasselhoff had to run over to check if he was OK, was beaten by the Argentinia winger who crossed for Crespo to faucet the ball into the unguarded score-zone.

But it wasn't long before Wayne Roonaldo's parelleling score, as he pounced on Robert O'Ayala's mistake to toe the ball home.

Walter Samuel put the Argentinias back in front just after half-time as all the British stars took a nap during a 30-yard kick-ball infringement, and it had looked to stay that way until Owen remembered he was on the field and head-kicked a couple of scores.

Elsewhere, Team USA – one of the top 10 nation franchises on Earth – were held to a one-to-one tie by Scotland – which isn't even a real country! How embarrassing!

Inside the first quarter, Christian Dailly (which is the name of a door-to-door religious magazine in Florida) shoved DaMarcus Beasley in the 18-yard zone and DaJosh Wolfe slotted in the 12-yard kick-ball punishment.

But the plucky Scots came back into the game when Andy Webster head-kicked a cross past DaKasey Keller and that's how it stayed.

Spain thumped someone called Slovakia five-to-one, with world-class Liverpool Reds star Garcia Luis being awarded a hat, while former Liverpool Reds star Vladimir Smicer kicked the only score as Czech won in Norway.

After all these games, a clearer picture of who can win World Cup XVIII is appearing. I reckon it's between six teams: Britain, Brazil, Team USA, France, Spain, China (they must be able to find 11 good soccerers in 2 billion people!).

November 14 — Roonaldo for Portugal? How ridiculous!

Manchester faces a franchise v federal war with the Portugalese head coach over the nationalist future of Cristiano Roonaldo.

As Roonaldo is yet to kick for Britain thanks to the incompetence of Sven Eriksson, Portugal has persuaded the wideout to become Portugalese. This means that he cannot ever kick for Britain and he'll have to grow his hair long and cover it in oil.

So despite the fact that he is British and his brother kicks for Britain, Cristiano will be part of the Portugal franchise in World Cup XVIII next year! Unbelievable, isn't it?

Sir Fergie is furious with this, insisting that the kicker only plays in one of their two exhibition games as they don't start until 9.15pm, which means they finish after his bed-time.

But Portugalese head coach Luis Felipe Scolari made him kick in the win over Croatia and plans to use him in the tough game against Britain's conquerers Norn Iron.

November 15 — Burton Albinos 2—1 Manchester

Manchester fell a further game behind the London Chelseas after picking up a humiliating loss to the Burton Albinos in the EPL.

We had to play the game with all our top national franchise kickers unavailable, while Gary Neville and Roy Keano are still on the Injured Reserve.

The game was the first to be played in the Albinos' new stadium. Gabriel Heinze (knee) and Lewis Saha (hamstring) missed out, while the stadium was officially opened by Sir Fergie after Brian Clough (death) was unavailable.

So while our best kickers, like Wayne Roonaldo, Eddie Vandersar and Timmy Howard, were away kicking for their birthplaces, Manchester were down to the bare bones for the game.

Unfairly, the Burton Albinos have not lost a single kicker to a nation-on-nation game, so we were under a great deal of pressure. And it told as we succumbed to yet another loss as the momentum picked up following the win over the London Chelseas vanished. The result may now have ended our hopes of grabbing second spot in the standings.

Andy Ducros's one-time no-bounce kick gave the Burton Albinos their first score. And Jon Shaw got a second with a superb 15-yard spinning top shot in the 52nd minute.

Markus Neumayr staked his claim for a starting roster spot with a fine kick-ball infringement score, but it proved too little too late.

Sir Fergie was furious after the game, complaining that the colours of the teams made it hard to spot the kickers. After all, all the Burton team were very pale with white hair and they clashed with the lines on the field.

November 16 — Manchester want to take Michael

Manchester will pay Michael Ballack 55 million English pounds to join the franchise.

Sir Fergie is concerned that the Bayern Munchers middleman is not interested in a move to the Nike Trafford Ballpark, so he will attempt to bribe him with a shedload of money, which would enable him to buy as much Weinerschnizel as he wants.

This would make the middleman the payingest kicker in the entire EPL, getting even more money than Frank Lampard, Ferdinand Rio or Eric Djemba-Djemba. He is widely regarded as the long-term answer to Roy Keano, although if that's the answer, I'm not entirely sure what the question is.

But German person Franz Beckenbauer insists Michael should say 'Ballacks' to Manchester and move to Realmadrid in free agency.

Beckenbauer, known as The Kaiser for his singing in the indie rock circles of northern England, reckons that moving to Manchester would be a backward step for the kicker.

Well, I don't care what he says. What does he know? What has he ever done in soccer? When he's kicked or coached at the top level, then he can start criticizing my franchise!

November 17 — Switzerland lose neutral tag

The final roster for World Cup XVIII has been completed following the play-off play-offs.

From Europe, Spain and the Czech Mates got through, while Switzerland got into their first ever war after getting past Turkey. They didn't look very neutral as the kicks started flying!

The Switzerlanders had got through to World Cup XVIII on alphabetical order after tieing 4–4 with Turkey after two games. But the Turkeys were not happy with this and former Aston Holiday Homes defenseman Alpay was seen getting into a hockey fight with one of the opponents, before Benjamin Huggel mistook one of Turkey's head coaches for the soccer ball and gave it a good volley.

A full-on tunnel fight ensued and it only ended when Switzerlander Stephane Gricht was taken to hospital after being kicked in the Alpines.

The leader of world soccer organization FISA,

Switzerlandish man Sepp Blatter, promised a completely fair and balanced investigation into the disturbances, saying: "We will act tough. I will make sure that whoever is responsible for this fight between the savages from Turkey and the choirboys of Switzerland gets severely punished."

Elsewhere, the tactic of tag-team soccer paid off as Trinidad and Tobago reached the post-season. Trinidad kicked in the first half and there were no scores, but when Tobago came out for the second period their freshness told, as they head-kicked the decisive score.

And finally, Australia reached World Cup XVIII after a 12-yard kick-ball challenge against Uruguay. They will be a real danger to Britain in the post-series in Germany next year, as they always beat Britain at every sport.

November 18 — Roy Keano: a tribute

I don't know what to say. The legend Roy Keano has left Manchester.

The middleman has finally had enough of the dictatorial ways of Sir Fergie, ruling Manchester like a tin-pot republic, and has decided to leave the Nike Trafford Ballpark.

Keano didn't originally want to be a soccerer, starting his career with the Cobh Ramblers, a group of old folk who enjoy wandering through the countryside. And his love of trees took him to the Nottingham Arboretums, where he took up soccer. Sir Fergie noticed how his rambling background helped him cover every blade of grass and he brought him to Manchester in 1993, the year after soccer went professional and the EPL was born.

He caused a huge controversy in 2001 when he admitted deliberately hurting Manchester team-mate Alf Haaland in an exhibition game between the starting roster and minor league side.

Keano has been one of the best middlemen in the EPL, but he somehow failed to get a call into the Britain nation roster. The call finally came in 2002 for the World Cup, but he walked out on the team after arguing with the head coach over who would win in an arm wrestle between Superman and The Fonz. He was never asked to play for Britain again and he missed the World Cup in 2003 and 2004.

Recently, he was taken to court after being accused of beating a 16-year-old kid with a bike chain, but the case was thrown out when Keano insisted he wouldn't need the bike chain.

The middleman was back in form this series, but his series was brought to a halt when his metatarsal split in two against the Liverpool Reds. He was expected back in January, but his time at Manchester has been brought to an end after the infamous interview with MUTV.

In the interview, he slated Darren Fletcher, Liam Miller, Jono Shea and Kerion Richardson, saying none of them are good enough to kick for Manchester. Sir Fergie was furious, not because he didn't agree with him, but because Keano had come up with better insults than he could. Personally, I think the kickers should count themselves lucky that he didn't wait for an exhibition game and tackle them knee-high.

That proved the last straw and Sir Fergie and Roy Keano have agreed a parting of the ways, supposedly by mutual consent. That smacks of a teenage boy who gets dumped by his girlfriend, then shouts, 'Yeah, well I'm leaving you too!'

I believe the Manchester team will wear black arm-bands in their game against the Charlton Addicts this weekend. Personally, I feel sorry for Keano's dog. Poor Fido has only just recovered from his post-2002 World Cup walkathon.

Meanwhile, it's been lost in the shock news of the day that there was *some* good news at the Nike Trafford Ballpark today. Cristiano Roonaldo has inked a new deal with Manchester to keep him at the franchise until 2010.

The wideout will now stay with his brother Wayne for the next five years, ending the rumors that Portugalese club Realmadrid and Spanish social inadequate franchise all the Barca Loners were interested in trading for him.

Cristiano has had a number of problems recently, but has overcome them to finally learn to write, which was enough to allow him to sign his name. He said: 'I am very happy and proud to finally put a signature on paper. It is important for my development.'

So at least something good happened today.

November 19 — Manchester face fears of addiction

Manchester fans have to run the gauntlet this weekend as they travel to Wales to face the Charlton Addicts in the Valley.

The game itself will be a tough one as the Addicts have already beaten the London Chelseas this series, but it is the road fans making the long trip that I worry about.

The Addicts are the soccer team of the local Outreach program, designed to wean people off their addictions and get them back into ordinary society. For example, Chris Perry can't stop chewing gum, Jerome Thomas needs help for his obsession with the books of JK Rowling and Radostin Kishishev is being treated for his addiction to washing machines.

But as well as the roster, the fans are from the program too and that could cause some problems in the stadium. I know that soccer fans have the reputation of being the best behaved fans in sport – none of that constant drinking and dressing up as the Pink Panther like rowdy trouble-making cricket fans do.

But some of the Addicts fans may make it difficult for Manchester's rooters. There is one famous fan who has an Obsessive Compulsive Disorder for cleaning and last week, he got someone thrown out of the stadium for dropping a Twix wrapper on the ground. And you know how Manchester fans like their shrimp sandwiches.

Meanwhile, there's another fan who is addicted to cow

tipping, a country game in which people pay for good service after cattle are taught silver service restaurant waitressing.

November 20 — Charlton Addicts 1—3 Manchester

That one's for Roy Keano! Manchester started their new era with a three-to-one win over the Charlton Addicts in the Valley in Wales.

The game will be remembered for two historic events. The first was the beginning of the post-Keano Manchester roster and the second was that Rude Nistelrooy kicked his first score from outside the 18-yard zone!

His 12 scores so far this series have come from a combined distance of 17 yards, so to double that in one go is an incredible achievement.

Before that, Alan Smith proved that he can be the new Keano – first with a thunderous late, high tackle, then with the opening score. Wayne Roonaldo crossed to Darren Fletcher, but the hapless middleman got his feet stuck in the turf, stumbled and did a messy forward roll. Smith, however, is full of hap and strode onto the loose ball, unleashing a fizzing drive that screamed into the lower third of the score-zone.

Yet somehow, the Addicts hit back against the run of the soccer ball. Darren Ambrose, spending a year at the Valley to attempt to get over his addiction to bubblewrap, swapped kicks with the Addicts' Bent offenser before curling the ball into the corner.

But it wasn't long before we retook the lead, thanks to Nistelrooy's masterpiece. He met Wayne Roonaldo's lofted pass with a chest-kick, before spinning and firing a ferocious air-kick-kick into the top corner.

He grabbed a second score inside the two-minute warning, sliding a tame kick past goaltender Stephan Andersen, who lucky for him is addicted to picking the soccer ball out of the net.

The win takes us to within a win of the Wigan Warriors in second position in the standings after they lost a three-to-two nailbiter to the London Arsenals. But can we do it and secure second spot without Roy Keano?

November 21 — The truth behind Roy Keano

I've had a couple of days to take in the shocking news that Roy Keano will never again wear the red shirt of Manchester, so I thought I should attempt to explain what happened.

Reports suggest that Keano was fired by Sir Fergie for questioning his authority, as the head coach decided he could no longer work with his captain. Here is a precise account of what took place over those fateful last few weeks at the Nike Trafford Ballpark.

November 1: Keano slams several of his team-mates in an interview that was banned from the franchise's own TV station. In the interview, Keano called Darren Fletcher 'Lurch', said Alan Smith 'smells of mushy peas', thought Liam Miller 'is better at crocheting than he is at soccer' and that Keiron Richardson 'has hair like one of those little troll dolls'.

November 4: Keano repeats his interview to the kickers in person, adding that Jono Shea was wearing a girl's tracksuit. When Sir Fergie threatened to set Carlos Quieroz on him, Keano replied: 'Quieroz couldn't win a fight. He's too defensive. He'd spend the whole time trying to block. How come he is your assistant coach anyway? He looks like one of the Munsters.'

November 17: Keano turns up at a Manchester minor league game to make his comeback from injury and is told that he is not on the roster. He suggests politely that perhaps the minor league coach should stick the roster in his cassocks, or something like that.

November 18: Keano and his lawyer attend a meeting with Sir Fergie where they are told that Keano will not be offered a new contract and will not be offensive captain any longer. Keano listens to Sir Fergie's criticisms calmly before telling Sir Fergie that he is going to do some origami with his butt, or something like that. Sir Fergie, now cowering in the corner, tells Roy that his services are no longer required and could he please clear his desk. Keano replied that he doesn't have a desk and if he did, Sir Fergie's head would be smashed repeatedly into it. He then went to hit Sir Fergie, but Quieroz quickly blocked his effort.

So a wonderful 12-year Manchester career ended just like that. It's a shame and there's going to be a big Keano-shaped hole at the Nike Trafford Ballpark for quite some time. Although that's because Keano stormed out through one of the walls, cartoon-style.

So which franchise should Keano miss games with a knee injury for? Here is my guide to his potential rosters.

Pompeii Pompeys

They were the first franchise to say they were interested in him and they could really do with his services. It would be pretty funny to watch him shouting at Laurent Robert as the moody Frenchman hits another 45-yard kick out of the ground (although to be fair, any shot missing the score-zone at the Pompeii Stadium goes out of the ground).

Glasgow-Ireland Greens

Keano's most likely destination, the franchise he supported as a boy. It means he'd be able to finish his career playing exhibition games against comedy franchises like Hibernian and the Partick Thistles. They are a bit like the Harlem Globetrotters – they mess about, but always end up winning in the end.

London Arsenals

People have criticized the London Arsenals for trading Irish middleman Paddy Vieira and they still need a replacement. Their treatment room is already pretty busy, so I'm not sure if there is space for Keano there.

Wigan Warriors

The rugby franchise would suit Keano as it would allow him to get rid of his frustration. Plus, he'd be moving to a better franchise. By the way, I think the Wigan Warriors are a rugby union franchise, rather than rugby league, which is a different sport. I'm not sure exactly what the difference is, but Pop tells me league has two less idiots.

Sunderland

I think Keano and Sunderland head coach Mick McCarthy are bound to get on well.

November 22 – Manchester in danger of breaking

Manchester face a make-or-get-broken game tonight when they meet the might of Real Villa at the Nike Trafford Ballpark.

We face the humiliation of being struck off from the Euro Series if we fail to win the game, but luckily, Real Villa have been deprived of their two top kickers.

Firstly and most importantly, Europe's top kicker Diego Forlan misses the chance to impress the Manchester trading staff after going on the Injured Reserve with a torn dreadlock.

Then Juan 'Roman' Riquelme hurt his upper leg muscle and will also miss the game. That is really good for Manchester as Riquelme was the MVP of Britain's recent three-to-two win over Argentina and he would have been a big danger to us. By the way, Riquelme's nickname is

Roman as he started life building really, really straight roads for a living.

More good news is that Gary Neville is back on the first-team roster and exected to replace Jono Shea in the Manchester defense. That will certainly add some stability to us as it's important to have the class prefect back in action.

It's not been the best week of preparation for Wayne Roonaldo though. The offenser was allegedly caught on CCTV camera kissing a girl that wasn't his girlfriend in a nightclub in Altrincham, a small town a long way from Manchester's home.

According to British newstabloid the *Sun*, Roonaldo apparently took a 'pretty brunette' into the kitchen of the club, then spotted the camera and covered it up. After that, enthusiastic grunting and slurping could be heard, presumably as Wayne discovered a meat pie in the fridge.

His girlfriend Colleen found out what happened and told Wayne he was in the 'last-chance saloon'. Let's hope there aren't any pretty brunettes in that saloon.

November 23 — Manchester 0—0 Real Villa

I said yesterday's game was a make-or-get-broken game. Well, it turns out it was a make-or-get-broken-or-nothing-much-will-happen game.

Manchester and Real Villa kicked out another zip-zip tie in the Euro Series' Group of Paint Drying. I didn't get to see the game, but I can confirm that the walls in the spare bedroom are dry and I probably had more fun than the people at the Nike Trafford Ballpark last night.

Real Villa were without their entire spine for the game, as their top goaltender, defenseman, middleman and offenser were all missing. But that didn't affect them too much. After all, Ferdinand Rio has been playing without his spine all year.

From what I can make out, nothing much happened. Wayne Roonaldo had a shot batted away by the Villas' goaltender, Park Ji-Sung got his kick blocked, while Rude

Nistelrooy decided to spend the majority of the game falling over, getting back up again and sighing.

At the other end of the field, Gary Neville made his return from the IR, replacing Wes Brown, who was tiring under the weight of his ginger afro. Meanwhile, Eddie Vandersar managed to catch up on a good deal of sleep, slumped up against the score-zone post.

This result – and the zip-zip tie between the Lille Savages and Ben Fica XI – means that we must get some kind of result from the last game of the series in the road trip to the Ficas and that isn't going to be easy.

Manchester haven't won in our last six proper Euro Series games – not including those joke ones when we kicked against teams from funny imaginary nations like Hungary and Romania. We haven't won on the road for two years now in Europe. Still, at least we can only get better as we meet these better franchises than us.

November 24 – Manchester logo-mate leaves

Manchester have lost their main jersey logo brand after Vodaphone decided not to continue their business with the franchise.

The UK company, who make cellphones and trombones, are fed up with the continued lack of success at the franchise under under-achieving head coach Sir Fergie and cut their deal short two years early. Their decision could cost Manchester 18 million English dollars.

Pop says they are only the second jersey logo Manchester have had following the 18-year deal we had with Sharp, who make kitchen knives and pointed sticks.

So who should Manchester get as their new uniform logo mate? I've looked at a few companies who would suit us perfectly.

Conservative Party – Popular in the south of Britain, but not in the north.

UK Independence Party – Seemingly hell-bent on getting out of Europe.

Cathedral City Blue Stilton Cheese – Crumbles easily under pressure.

Wernham Hogg – Great potential, but let down by a terrible boss.

Tatton Park Flower Show – In the shadow of the Chelseas version in London.

Krispy Kreme Donuts – Soft in the centre.

O2 – Would be a huge coup to steal the logo from rivals the London Arsenals, but would also represent 'oh and two', our recent road record in the Euro Series.

Meanwhile, Manchester have insisted that they would not be changing the name of their stadium as part of the new sponsorship package. And quite right . . . why would we want to change the name of the Nike Trafford Ballpark?

November 25 — Thanksgiving

It was Thanksgiving in the States yesterday – the day when we all spend time with our families and talk about all the things we are grateful for during the past year.

Mom made a lovely great meal, finding a turkey that looked like Darren Fletcher (although I don't think that was too tricky). The pumpkin for the pie also had a close resemblance to Wayne Roonaldo after a sunbed.

Then we all went around the table, giving thanks for everything good that happened in the last 12 months. Pop was thankful that Mom never found out about the time he let me taste beer. Mom was grateful that she secretly knows everything and that I didn't like the taste of beer. Me – I'm thankful to all my readers, for Eddie Vandersar's goaltending skills and the fact that I never bumped into Roy Keano in a dark alley.

But I wonder what happened around the Glaz-meister's dinner table last night? Here are the things that Super Malcolm and Manchester are thankful for this year.

- The ginger leprechaun beard is coming back into fashion for the winter season.

- Cristiano Roonaldo has been told he will not be charged with rapping this week. He had insisted that he was innocent, claiming that he was actually singing Phil Collins, although many people believe that is a criminal offense anyway.
- Kleberson likes warm weather.
- Sir Fergie no longer takes practice on Thursdays, as he has to queue up in the Post Office to pick up his Giro.
- Wayne Roonaldo hasn't been asked to appear on Play the Pundit on MUTV yet.
- We can't fail to get a win this weekend, as Roy Carroll is the Western Hammers goaltender.
- Someone finally found Liam Miller under some towels in a cupboard and shipped him off to the Leeds Enrons.

November 26 — George Best — a tribute

Former Manchester star George Best has died, aged 59.

Best suffered multiple organ failure following internal bleeding, after being admitted to the Cromwell Hospital in London – close to the Nike Trafford Ballpark – on October 1 with flu symptoms.

The hospital did all they could to keep him alive, giving him a blood transfusion. He got 40 pints in 10 hours, which beat his record by about 10 minutes.

The legend, who once said 'Half of my money I spend on women and liquor, the rest I just spent on medical bills,' is survived by his girlfriend Ros and son Calum, who has made a pledge that as a tribute to his father, he will sleep with as many beautiful women as possible.

Best is famous for the amount of alcohol he was able to consume and the amount of Miss Worlds he was able to consume. He gave up liquor a couple of years ago, but only when he was asleep.

Best kicked for Manchester for 11 years from 1963 until 1974, before the EPL was formed, when franchises kicked against anyone they could find as there wasn't any kind of league. He kicked 178 scores for us, although six came in one game against the Northampton Nils, so that hardly counts.

In 2000, he came second in a poll to find the greatest Manchester kickers ever, behind Eric Canton. Although, in a poll last week, he came second behind Roy Keano. And in a poll I read today, Best has been upgraded to number one in the list with 96% of the vote. I'm sure if he ever did any paintings, they will have tripled in price in the last day.

After getting sacked by Manchester for drinking Babycham out of the Euro Series trophy, he drifted from franchise to franchise, kicking for the Fulham Fayeds, San Jose Earthquakes, Los Angeles Aztecs and the Alabama Alcoholics. Best says he learnt a lot during his time in America. Mainly, I assume, eating burgers and swearing on chat shows.

Pop says it was Best coming over to America that got him into soccer in the first place. He went to see him when Best kicked against the Tampa Bay Rowdies, but was disappointed to find him incoherent and swaying. Then Best decided to start drinking.

Best was also sentenced to a three-month spell at the Blackburn Pyros for drunk driving, assaulting a police officer and drinking a policeman's pepper spray. He had to spend Christmas 1984 behind bars and he made up for it since then by spending every Christmas behind a bar.

November 27 — Western Hammers 1—2 Manchester

Wayne Roonaldo was the inspiration as Manchester ensured they got a zip-to-three point turnaround win at the Western Hammers.

It was an especially sweet one for Ferdinand Rio, who kicked against his little brother Anton Rio for the first time since he was 10 and got ejected from their games lesson for giving Anton a wedgie.

During the planned minute's silence for the late, great George Best, disrespectful fans clapped throughout and sang

Best's name. That appalling behavior clearly got to Manchester and we made the worst start possible. Well, the worst start possible would be to get lost on the short journey to the Hammers' Toolbox Stadium and get bus-jacked, only turning up with two minutes to spare, having to play in our vests and underpants, but you know what I mean.

With over 89 minutes still on the clock, the Western Hammers kicked the go-ahead score while some of the Manchester roster were still tying their cleat laces. It was a swift drive upfield by the Hammers as Matthew Etherington sprinted down the sideline and sent a perfect ball for Marlon Hare-Wood to divert smartly inside the near vertical bar.

Manchester had chance after chance to get back into it, but found ex-goaltender Roy Carroll having his one good performance of the year. He made great blocks from Rude Nistelrooy, Wayne Roonaldo and Paul Scholes (a rare kick at the score-zone for the defensive middleman).

Things weren't looking good for us and Michael Silvester was so out of his depth in the game that he was given some inflatable armbands to play in before he was eventually replaced with someone better.

The pressure told in the end as Roonaldo got the breakthrough, thumping the ball into the scoring-zone off Carroll's foot shortly after half-time. And Jono Shea completed the loss-to-win spin as he leapt higher than the goaltender to head-kick his first score of the series.

In the end, it could have been more decisive and Nistelrooy was unlucky not to get on the scorer list as he turned and sent a wonderful french fry over Carroll and on to the horizontal bar.

Manchester's entire roster celebrated the win, which moved them into second placing in the EPL standings – ahead of the London Arsenals and Wigan Warriors. Except Ferdinand Rio, who sought out Anton and got him in a headlock before locking him in the cupboard under the stairs for a couple of hours.

November 28 – The future without Sir Fergie

It's time to take a step back and look at what is going on at Manchester and I have a worrying feeling that Manchester's no-pennant era is going to be extended for quite a while.

First, our top kicker Roy Keano gets sacked for telling the truth (it's lucky that Wayne Roonaldo is such a liar), and now, it is becoming clear that Sir Fergie has no plans to quit. What a disaster.

Most people thought that Manchester would have a new head coach next year – one that gives us at least a small hope of winning at least something. But Sir Fergie insists he is going to ensure that Manchester remain winless for at least the next four years. FOUR YEARS? The London Chelseas will be 15 wins better than us every series.

He claimed that retirement was 'definitely not on the agenda', so let's hope the Glaz-meister is clever enough to sneak it into Any Other Business.

But despite this, there is slight hope as people are talking about who could replace Sir Fergie when he eventually is impeached. The British news tabloids were saying that Roy Keano is keen to return to the Nike Trafford Ballpark in the head role.

One man even claims Manchester has offered him a job. Otto Hitzfeld. Now, getting rid of Sir Fergie is what all Manchester fans want, but I'm not entirely sure this Otto guy is the right replacement.

Yes, he has won the Euro Series twice, once with the Bayern Munchers and once with some other team sometime last millennium, but he has been unemployed for two years. He's probably been sitting around at home on his butt watching *Sunset Beach*, only leaving the house to pick up his unemployment benefit, then spending it all at the bookmakers. (To find out what the British newspapers are saying, I've been reading the *Daily Mail*. Is it showing?)

He can't even speak English! I mean who doesn't know how to speak English? Except Wayne Roonaldo obviously.

And soccer has changed a lot in the time that he has been away. Pop says that they never used to have a no-back-pass rule and the ball used to be made out of a youth team kicker's stomach.

Still, after Otto's steered the franchise to new heights, like the quarter-finals of the Euro Series, then Roy Keano can take over and win us the Euro Series. Although by the time we do that, Wayne's son might be kicking for Manchester!

November 29 — Manchester's rivals losing the plot

I might be getting ahead of myself, but I have a sneaking suspicion that Manchester might – just might – be in with a chance of winning the EPL pennant. This is mainly because our local rivals are starting to lose the plot.

Really strange things are happening at the London Arsenals. Firstly, there is a lot of talk that Thierry Henry is strongly disliked by the other players because he is too good and they might have to send him over to the Barca Loners for a while. And head coach Arsene Wenger may be in trouble because he is a witness for a car accident, yet when the police spoke to him, he insisted: 'I did not see the incident.'

And now I see that the franchise's Singaporian wideout Freddie Liung Berg was on the Injured Reserve with a sore knee, so the medical staff decided to take his wisdom teeth out!

Actually, thinking about that, it's not too uncommon. At my school, one of the kids had a headache and the Principal gave him a thorough prostate examination.

Meanwhile, things are starting to go wrong at the London Chelseas. The franchise has been fined over 50,000 English dollars by the Soccer Association for problems with their fans during a Carl Ing Tribute Cup game last series. That's going to make a hole in their finances when they try to add to their roster in January!

In more good news, Manchester's next opponents the

146

Pompeii Pompeys are without a head coach and trying to tempt Scotch League franchise the Glasgow Rule Britannias' leader Alex McLeish, a man who has managed to get his team to fourth position in a two-horse race. With him in charge, we can't fail to win!

November 30 — Rossi the runt of the litter

Sir Fergie has strongly criticized Manchester's star youngster Giuseppe Rossi.

The American legend, who could go on to be the most capped kicker for the United States ever in the 13-year history of soccer, has already kicked two scores for Manchester, as well as 14 in 13 games this series for the minor, minor league team (including, bizarrely, earning a hat for three kick-scores against our minor league team's minor league team). Yet Sir Fergie reckons he won't get many more.

Our head coach said that Rossi was just as good a score-kicker as Paul Scholes is. So we can expect Rossi not to get on the scorers-paper for the next nine months and to pick up lots of yellow pieces of paper from the referee.

Why is Sir Fergie hammering our best rookie? Has he got to the stage that he just wants to get fired now or is he just becoming more incompetent as each day goes by?

Anyway, I don't suppose Rossi will be in the Manchester roster for the Carl Ing Tribute Cup 1/8 final clash with the Western Bromwiches. Rude Nistelrooy and Wayne Roonaldo will continue the partnership that impressed in Wales at the Western Hammers, while Wayne's brother Cristiano will be hoping for a recall.

Sir Fergie rested all his starting rotation in the last two rounds. We even saw the minor league side lose to the Doncaster Osmonds in the first round, but the SA decided to let us back into the pennant as we were struggling so much. But I can't imagine he will cut kickers for this game. After all, we are only three wins from a Bowl game and the chance of our first pennant for years.

Only someone who knows nothing about soccer would give all our top kickers a rest tonight.

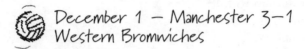 December 1 – Manchester 3–1 Western Bromwiches

Sir Fergie gave some of our top kickers a rest tonight. Luckily he realized that this is the only chance we have of winning a pennant, so he did play a very strong team anyway.

Rude and Wayne were missing, but Cristiano returned and super Keiron Richardson and even superer Timmy Howard both got well-deserved spots on the starting roster.

Luckily, it was enough to get past the Western Bromwiches and into the quarter-finals of the Carl Ing Tribute Cup. With the London Chelseas already out of this competition after they ran away from the scary Charlton Addicts, it gives us a great chance of going all the way to the Carl Ing Cup.

Early on, Cristiano Roonaldo proved he is learning a lot from his brother with a dive to win a 12-yard kick-ball punishment. He got up, dusted himself down and shuffled himself sideways to kick Manchester into the lead.

Lewis Saha, returning from a long game of hide and seek with Liam Miller, then got his first score since January, a record that makes Paul Scholes look proficient. Saha fired a kick straight at Bromwiches' goaltender Russell Hoult, but the ball moved in the air (how can a ball not move in the air, unless David Copperfield is making it levitate) and it snuck into the score-zone.

Then Manchester's new star offenser Jono Shea got on the scorers-paper with his second in two games. Swapping kicks with Saha, he controlled the ball with a chest-kick before firing an unstoppable shot to make it three-zip. I think there is little doubt that Shea is the future of Manchester's offensive line and the sooner Sir Fergie plays him instead of

Rude, the better.

As predicted, Sir Fergie has ruined awesome American Giuseppe Rossi. After he compared him to Paul Scholes, Rossi succeeded in not getting any scores. Why couldn't he have compared him to Jono Shea?

Still, we are in the last eight teams, with giants the London Arsenals, Wigan Warriors and Doncaster Osmonds still in the pennant. It's going to be tough, but I reckon we could be finally on for a return to pennant-winning ways in the Glaz-meister's first series in charge!

December 2 — Ole to come in from the cold

Manchester's misfiring offenser Ole Solskjaer could be set for a shock return to the Manchester minor, minor league side for the clash with the Liverpool Reds on Monday.

Solskjaer has not kicked a score since September 2003 – 26 months!!! – and not in the EPL since April that year, making Paul Scholes seem like a score-kicking machine like Pele or Jono Shea. Yet Sir Fergie is so desperate for scores with Rude Nistelrooy looking out of form that he has turned to the wasteful Norwegian.

Solskjaer is now in contention to partner Wayne Roonaldo in the offense for the crucial Euro clash with the Ben Fica XI.

It is another sign that Sir Fergie is losing it. Only last week, he told anyone who would listen to him that he would never place Solskjaer on the roster again. So his U-turn shows just how desperate the Manchester head coach has become.

Solskjaer did get one of the most important scores in Manchester's history, knee-kicking the hurt-addition time score as we beat the Bayern Munchers in the Euro Series final. Unfortunately, that score was a long time ago now ... sometime last millennium.

Sir Fergie has even paved the way for his return by stripping Rude Nistelrooy of the Manchester captaincy. Gary

Neville will wear the armband for Saturday's game against the Pompeii Pompeys, while in the last two games, the roster shared being captain as they all had black armbands on.

Neville was chosen ahead of Ryan Giggs, which is kind of obvious. How is Ryan going to tell people what to do from the substitutes' bench?

December 3 — Manchester 3–0 Pompeii Pompeys

Manchester stormed back to second spot in the EPL after a three-zip win over the Pompeii Pompeys at the Nike Trafford Ballpark.

The Pompeys looked extremely tired, probably due to their 1,000-mile trip from Southern Italy and they were never really in the game. To be honest, I think a lot has changed in soccer since ancient times and perhaps Pompeii are no longer suited to the EPL.

It became a very historic day as well, as Paul Scholes got his first score in living memory. In fact, the last time he did find the score-zone, you could only see it in black and white, although that suited him as you couldn't tell he was ginger. The middleman had so much space in the Pompeii 18-yard zone that he was able to turn it into a loft-conversion. He also rose high to head-kick Ryan Giggs's corner ball into the bottom corner.

This game was so easy that Sir Fergie decided to put just three defensemen on the roster, with four middlemen and three offensers – Wayne Roonaldo, Rude Nistelrooy and Jono Shea. Unfortunately, Shea had to be put on the Injured Reserve during the half-time show and had to be replaced. How do you hurt yourself during half-time? Maybe he choked on his Earl Grey or Sir Fergie was doing his hairdryer thing and accidentally nipped the top of his ear with his scissors.

Losing our top offenser affected the team and we struggled a bit in the second period, only adding to our scores in the last 10 minutes. First Roonaldo continued his hot score streak, which started in a nightclub in Altrincham, with a fierce kick from 20 yards. Then Rude added a third score late on as he lofted the ball over Pompeii goaltender Frankie Howerd.

Our bid for second position in the standings received a huge boost as, elsewhere in the EPL, the London Arsenals picked up a loss in the Wall Game with posh private school the Boltonians thanks to scores from Abdoulaye Faye and Easyjet entrepreneur Stelios.

And at the Liverpool Reds, Peter Crouch finally got around to looking up the word 'score' in the dictionary and managed to kick 1.5 scores in the very impressive three-zip win over the Wigan Warriors.

December 4 — Keano interested in Manchester return?

Roy Keano is still deciding which franchise he would like to take a downwards step to following his awesome career at Manchester. And the really shock news is that one of the favorites to draft Keano is . . . Manchester!

The legendary middleman, last seen walking his dog for the seventh time in one day, is currently mulling over offers from franchises the length and breadth of the lower end of the EPL.

Teams who are already facing a series of mediocrity and boredom – such as the Boltonians and the Western Hammers, have expressed an interest in Keano, hoping that at least he'll slag his team-mates off again, which would give them something to talk about.

But now, Sir Fergie has attempted to deliver the ultimate snub to Manchester's greatest ever kicker – or second or third best, depending on when you read the poll. Our evil head coach wants to re-sign (don't get excited readers – that says Sir Fergie wants to re-sign, not resign) Keano and dump him in our minor league roster!

The minor league roster are surprisingly second favorites to ink a deal with the middleman, perhaps paving the way for his return to the Nike Trafford Ballpark. He still loves the franchise, it's just that, like so many of us, he hates Sir Fergie. Once the coach leaves, he can come back and play for us again.

Even in five years' time, he would still be able to get on the Manchester roster, as Darren Fletcher is still likely to be making his runs down the sideline into soccer cul-de-sacs.

Meanwhile, David Beckham says he would welcome Roy Keano at Realmadrid, presumably because he needs a bodyguard over there in Portugal.

December 5 — Manchester to face bogey franchise

Manchester could have to kick against bogey franchise the Burton Albinos in the first stage of the SA Super Bowl. We must face our demons if the Albinos can overcome the Burs Coughs in the pre-first round clash tomorrow.

As I'm sure you remember, Manchester suffered a humiliating two to one loss to the Albinos during the last nation-on-nation super clash calendar gap section and I'm dreading the thought of having to kick against them again. The game would be played at the Albinos' Pirelli Stadium, which has a slick surface.

The Albinos are head coached by the legendary Brian 'Nigel' Clough, who coached the Nottingham Arboretums to two Euro Series triumphs, although, to be fair, they were in the 1980s, when only Britain played soccer anyway. Brian is nicknamed Nigel as he is continually making plans for himself.

Amongst their famous current roster are former Macclesfield Worms legend Darren Tinson, as well as Silas from the *Da Vinci Code*, whose bio says he is an assassin, so he must be excellent at finishing his scores.

I really hope the Coughs win tomorrow night, but even

they will prove a tough franchise to beat. After all, they have won the Lancashire Evening Post Sunday League Youth Division Championship pennant and League Cup Bowl for the last two years in a row!

December 6 — Manchester prepare for win-or-don't-win clash

Manchester has a win-or-don't-win game tomorrow as we aim to get through to the next round of the Euro Series.

A win on the road at the Ben Fica franchise would take us into the second round (it's the second round even though we've already kicked eight full games – you crazy Europeans) and would equal the furthest that Manchester has reached in the pennant for years.

We're even helped by the fact that the Ben Fica XI are so stricken with injuries, illnesses and kickers with notes from their Mom excusing them from action that we will actually be coming up against the Ben Fica VIII.

They are missing Simmow, who kicked the 20-yard wavy kick-ball infringement kick-score in the first game between these franchises at the Nike Trafford Ballpark, offenser Miccoli and wideout Karagounis, who is out with a hair strain – a problem that affects a lot of Greek kickers as they normally have more hair than most.

Sir Fergie believes Manchester will be inspired by George Best for this game. I can only assume he means that it will make the kickers want to win even more than ever, otherwise they could turn to drink and not end up reaching their full potential. On an entirely unrelated note, I see that Paul Gazza has been sacked as manager of a franchise called the Ketter Rings.

If we do lose tomorrow, we will be out of the Euro Series and Sir Fergie will probably be cut by the Glaz-meister. So although this is a make-or-break game for Manchester, it's a make-or-make one for us big Manchester fans. After all, we either get through or we get rid of our head coach!

December 7 — Ben Fica VIII 2—1 Manchester

I said it was a make-or-break game for Manchester. Well it turns out it was a make-or-go-broke game. And make is outta town – along with all the decent soccer kickers.

Manchester were knocked out of the Euro Series

 Wednesday, costing Super Malcolm 20 million English dollars. Of course, that's small change for him, but as the saying goes, 'Take care of the millions and the billions will take care of themselves.'

Sir Fergie has let the Glaz-meister down and he must pay for it. Preferably, he will be cut as manager, but at the very least, for a punishment, he should be made to hand over his favorite things – his supply of whisky and nose-blusher.

And yet, for a while, everything was on course. Paul Scholes continued his magical series as he grabbed a shin-kick score just 6 minutes in. After Cristiano Roonaldo's center, Scholes got his cleat stuck in the mud and bundled the soccer ball, himself, the goaltender and a dwarf into the score-zone. Oh no, Scholes was the dwarf.

But our joy lasted for just 10 minute as maestro Giovanni dived in at the far vertical bar, as Ferdinand Rio stood around trying to get the dirt out of his fingernails.

And then the Ben Fica VIII sealed their come-from-a-score-down-and-go-a-score-up victory to leave Sir Fergie red-faced – although that's not entirely unexpected. Beto had a speculative kick from 20 yards which Eddie Vandersar would have easily batted away, but Scholes is in such hot score-kicking form, that he couldn't stop himself and deliberately turned it into the score-zone.

From then on, nothing seemed to happen. Wayne Roonaldo did his best, but even he needs some help. Quite simply we were not good enough and some players didn't perform. I know that the Ben Fica goaltender was big, but he wasn't that scary. Yet Roonaldo seemed terrified by the sight of Quim.

The sooner we get rid of the perennially under-achieving Sir Fergie the better. We have never and will never win anything with him as head coach.

December 8 — Who should replace Sir Fergie?

The fallout from our Euro Series exit has begun. Having thought about it, it isn't that bad. It could have been a lot worse. After all, we could have ended up getting into the next round of the UESA Cup. Now that would have been humiliating.

Sir Fergie has been told that he will be cut if Manchester doesn't win the EPL, so with us four wins behind the London Chelseas already, he is as good as gone.

Obviously Sir Phelan is everyone's choice for his replacement, being our winningest coach, but he probably doesn't want to leave the job where he is so successful. So with the help of Pop and Mister Internet, I have put together a short list for Super Malcolm Glazer to look over and select a new leader.

Stuart Pearce

He led our minor league side to a famous tie against our starting roster, so he is clearly a talented head coach. He has a bit of a psycho side, so the kickers will be used to working with someone like him after all that time with Sir Fergie.

Roy Keano

There's nothing that this legend of Manchester can't do (except control his temper). This would make him an ideal replacement for Sir Fergie, although there is the chance he would fall out with himself and refuse to turn up for a game. I don't think Darren Fletcher wants him to get the job though.

Fabio Capello

An Italian model-turned-head-coach with an extensive knowledge of brown shoes. Being Italian, his expertise on hair products will help make a smooth transition from Sir Fergie and his hairdryer.

Iain Dowie

Jose Mourinho is the Special One, but he would be unavailable, so the next best man is Dowie, who looks special, although perhaps not in the same way.

Carlton Palmer

He's available, which is probably the only thing he has going for him.

Steve Nicol

He's the head coach of the New England Revolution, who won the MLS Super Cup pennant, after topping the Eastern AA league. Despite being American, he has extensive knowledge of the British league after playing for the Liverpool Reds in the pre-EPL conference in the 1980s.

A spokesman for the Glazer triplets insisted that they were not panicking about the loss and just because they are not talking about it, doesn't mean they don't know what is going on.

The spokesman said: 'Because they don't court the media, the assumption is of pygmies, out of their depth, naively expecting treble after treble.' I think that's harsh. Firstly, there is a big difference between a pygmy and a leprechaun. And secondly, if they are out of their depth, they aren't expecting trebles, they're expecting lifejackets.

Meanwhile, Manchester's kickers have labelled Cristiano Roonaldo a showpony following his showing off exhibition against the Ben Fica VIII on Wednesday. When a replacement came on for Ryan Giggs, the angry Brit pointed at Roonaldo and screamed at Sir Fergie, 'Why are you taking me off? What about him?'

Everyone else was furious with Roonaldo as well, except Rude Nistelrooy, who was delighted that someone else was being compared to a horse for once.

December 9 — Britain given World Cup assignment

Britain have been given a tough run to the World Cup finals in 2006. Having failed to get through to the 2003, 2004 and 2005 competitions, it was always going to be difficult for Sven Eriksson's roster and so it proved.

We must play against Sweden, Paraguay, Trinidad and Tobago, in what will be known as, while not the group of death, certainly the group of a migraine and sore hip. This is what I have found out about the nations so far.

Sweden

Pop says Britain people have a stiff upper lip and they don't like coming up against Sweden, the only nation franchise to kick naked and they have a stiff something else.

Social reject Henrik Larsson of the Barca Loners and Zlatan Ibrahimovic, the Soviet-born offenser, will both be dangerous. But I would imagine that they will struggle in the stifling heat of the German climate next summer.

Trinidad and Tobago

Imagine if franchises played with their neighbours, like Britain and France or Portugal and Angola. That is what Britain are up against, when they take on both Trinidad AND Tobago in one game.

The Caribbean duo must surely start as the favorites for the group, especially as former Manchester legend Dwight Yorke is their star kicker. I'm not sure in what country Yorke is playing at the moment, but I understand he was in Jordan for a while.

Paraguay

Historically, a nation that is enemies with Britain, this will be a very difficult game. They tried to blow up London once and their country in English means 'For Guy', named after the man that tried to do it, Guy Faulkes.

Their best kicker is defensive hardman Carlos 'The Tackle' Gamarra, who managed to get through four full games in 1998 without conceding a single kick-ball infringement. So he's clearly not that hard then, if he can't even kick an offenser properly.

Four years ago, they could do everything except kick scores and only had one good kicker, Jose Chilavert, who had to be goaltender, 12-yard kick-ball kicker and middleman area anchorman all at the same time.

Team USA also have a tough group, after being scheduled to play against Italy, the nation that invented soccer after someone suggested their country looked a bit like a soccer cleat. Team USA also kick against the Czech Mates and Ghana, who have the London Chelseas star Michael Essien playing for them. I imagine Ghana are used to playing with a bigger soccer ball as Essien keeps on missing the ball and kicking opponents just above the knee.

December 10 — Land of the Rising Reds

Manchester's bid for second is looking up after the London Arsenals lost yet again.

This time, it was to the Newcastle Stripers, thanks to a score from Geordie Nobby Solano with nine minutes on the clock. Arsenals middleman Gilbert O'Silva was ejected, meaning that he now gets to go home to Tipperary for the Christmas period instead of having to kick.

But while they look like they will be competing with the Charlton Addicts for that all-important sixth spot, it seems the Liverpool Reds are our biggest challengers now for the first losers' spot. They have won seven EPL games in a row and haven't lost any scores since 1996.

And as they are the top franchise in Europe, they have been selected to head off to Japan to compete in the World Franchise Championship against the best rosters in the world, such as Costa Rican pennant winners' Deportivo Saprissa and Egypt the Al Ahly Pyramids.

It will be a huge step up in class for the Reds and I can't believe they can come out of this with any wins. They are more likely to come back with food poisoning from all the raw fish than with a pennant.

It's been a difficult week for Manchester, after getting kicked out of Europe – although that was not entirely unexpected. After all, we've been kicked out of Europe every year for ages!

Luckily, the EPL schedule has been kind to us and we will get back to winning ways tomorrow against the Everon Stickies, who we beat two-zip on Opening Day.

The franchise, from the town of Everton, were only one place below Manchester in the standings last series, but have struggled this time around, currently sitting in 17th spot, just below the Western Bromwiches.

I was trying to work out why they are doing so badly this year and I think I've worked it out. The only difference between their roster last series and this series is the addition of Phil Neville. The reason they are in the demotion spots is Phil Neville.

With him on the roster, we can't fail to get a win.

December 11 – Manchester 1–1 Everton Stickies

Manchester failed to get a win Sunday, as we were held to a one-one tie by the Everton Stickies.

Sir Fergie's grip on the coaching reins must be even looser, following the latest humiliation against a franchise that is in the bottom three spots in the EPL standings.

It could have been even worse though after we slipped into a losing position early in the game when James McFadden kicked from a really tight angle. But Pop tells me that Scotch people are good at being tight – and his kick whizzed in between Eddie Vandersar and the vertical bar, into the net, taking Sir Fergie closer to being fired before you could say Capello.

We got the parallel score when Paul Scholes lofted a kick over the Stickies' defensemen, who were glued to the spot, and Ryan Giggs tucked into the score-zone.

But after that, we couldn't find a way past the Stickies' back-up stopper Richard Wright. Wayne Roonaldo should have kicked two scores, but decided to miss on purpose as he is a Stickies fan.

It's lucky really that the Everton Stickies didn't have their scoring cleats on, as James Beattie missed an open score-zone and McFadden kicked easily at Vandersar when through. But then that is their problem. They were originally called the Stickies because they couldn't hit a piñata with a stick.

December 12 — Carlos the Tackle

There has been a lot of talk about what is the problem with Manchester at the moment.

Most fans think Sir Fergie is to blame – and for the most part, they are correct. The man knows very little about soccer, judging by his roster selections.

But I think there is another culprit at Manchester . . . Carlos Quieroz. The man is clearly extremely talented as a head coach. He used to have the job at Realmadrid in his native Portugal and you don't get that position by being bad.

But he simply doesn't stand up to Sir Fergie enough. He needs to tell him where he's going wrong: that all the top franchises like the London Chelseas and the Boltonians start with a five-kicker middleman area, meaning they have an extra man to kick opponents. It's what the fans want.

He needs to tell Sir Fergie that Jono Shea is our best offenser after Wayne Roonaldo. And he needs to tell him that when he is giving the hairdryer treatment, he should wait until Wes Brown's hair is dry, as that ginger afro is helping nobody.

Only then will he be able to finally end this pennant-less period and turn Manchester into a major force in British soccer.

The fans are even starting to get on Cristiano Roonaldo's case as well, but I think that's unfair. It's been a difficult few weeks for him. He is recovering from losing his father and he had that trouble with the police a few weeks ago.

Everyone knew he was innocent of the charges brought against him. How can he even have made a pass at a girl? No one has seen him make any kind of pass since he arrived at the Nike Trafford Ballpark.

December 13 — Wayne needs his beauty sleep

I think the pressure is finally getting to Wayne Roonaldo.

He says that when things are getting too much for him and after another Manchester defeat, he just wants to stay in bed all day. Although he was a sulky teenager until a couple of months ago, so that's not a huge surprise.

But he does say he forces himself out of bed to go and walk the dog. I'm a little confused though, as he doesn't actually have a dog. Unless he's talking about Colleen.

Wayne also insists there is no crisis at Manchester. But I looked up crisis in the dictionary and discovered it means: 'An unstable condition, as in political, social, or economic affairs, involving an impending abrupt or decisive change.' I'm not sure anyone would be complaining if there was a crisis if it means the impending abrupt and decisive change of our head coach.

We come up against the Wigan Warriors tomorrow night and luckily, they are in a worse streak than we are, having picked up four straight losses, sliding from second in the standings to seventh. Hopefully Wayne will get out of bed for the game. Maybe we can tempt him to the Nike Trafford Ballpark by leaving a trail of meat pies from his house.

December 14 — Sir Fergie fumes at press

Sir Fergie has let rip at the British tabloids, claiming it is their fault that Manchester are in their current slump.

The Manchester head coach had set up an interview with

all the papers all at once, but stormed out after just 74 seconds after they started asking questions.

Sir Fergie says the sports writers are entirely to blame, causing the fans to jeer the franchise on a regular basis by making stuff up. Maybe if they are making stories up, it turns out that it isn't true that he has let Roy Keano – our best kicker ever – leave.

Perhaps it will turn out that Sir Fergie is right – maybe it is the newspapers' fault after all. Perhaps it was the press that drafted Kleberson, Liam Miller and David Bellion. They then traded away Keano, David Beckham and Jaap Stam. And they then refused to quit to let Sir Phelan take control of the wayward franchise.

And to be fair, it's not a huge surprise. Sir Fergie seems to hold a grudge against Roy Keano, every referee ever except the one with the eyes, the entire British Broadcasting Company and any multi-millionaires who give him a free horse.

December 15 – Manchester 4–0 Wigan Warriors

Ferdinand Rio grabbed his first score for Manchester as we brushed aside the Wigan Warriors to hop back to second spot in the standings.

Rio finally got around to showing us some of his samba skills as he head-kicked Ryan Giggs's center-ball to get us off the mark. But the clear MVP was Wayne Roonaldo, who managed to get what the reports have called 'a brace' of scores. What kind of phrase is 'a brace'? Sounds like a brace of balls to me.

His first was a touch lucky, as he slipped over in the 18-yard zone – something he must have learnt from his brother – but it confused the Warriors' defenseman and he had time to get up and bury the ball past the goaltender.

If the first was messy, the second was pure EPL class as Rude Nistelrooy followed up his first 20-yard score with his first ever assist! He is becoming an all-rounder who can do everything. He will be unstoppable. Roonaldo sprinted on to his passed kick and sent a delightful french fry over goaltender Pollitt.

In between, he could have kicked another as he knocked the soccer ball against the horizontal bar from just two yards out, which for him must have been as annoying as when he spilt the filling of a meat pie down his top.

Rude added his standard 12-yard kick-ball punishment score late on, after winning it himself, rounding off a convincing win and unfortunately, easing the pressure on Sir Fergie.

Let's face it – it was an easy, easy win and it was very clear that Paul Jewell's franchise are really a rugby team. Especially as they spent the majority of the game kicking the ball way over the horizontal bar.

At the end, the emperor Ferg was happy, while there was a philosophical Jewell, which sounds a bit like a storyline from a Harry Potter book.

December 16 — Keano completes Ireland move

Roy Keano has completed a trade to the Glasgow-Ireland Greens.

Manchester's former offensive captain is set to join the franchise he rooted for as a youngster, but seeing he grew up in England, I'm not sure why he didn't follow a proper team.

Apparently, the franchise's owner Desmond Dermott is set to pay Keano's wages out of his own pocket, making him the first kicker to be officially owned by another person since Rude Nistelrooy was owned by Realvilla defenseman Javi Venta for 90 minutes.

After the Greens announced the deal, they unveiled him, presumably by pulling a sheet from over the top of him, and he got a chance to talk to the press for the first time since Keano Plays the Pundit.

In the interview, he called Manchester's kickers soft, said they no longer wanted to be pushed as hard as they could and called Paul Scholes a red dwarf.

It's good news as it means that Keano will not come back to the Nike Trafford Ballpark this series. He would run riot against middlemen like Darren Fletcher.

Despite Keano joining an Irish franchise, it is not known whether he has any Irish blood in him.

December 17 — Aston Holiday Homes 0–2 Manchester

Manchester ensured a win-win series against the Aston Holiday Homes as we eased to a two-zip win.

We are now just three wins behind the London Chelseas and as they kick against the London Arsenals tomorrow, we could make up one of those.

Again it was our Hollywood pairing of Wayne Roonaldo and Rude Nistelrooy (i.e. Shrek and Donkey) who made the difference, kicking the scores to take us to the win.

Nistelrooy got the first inside the opening 10 minutes, advancing on to what reports have called 'a Darren Fletcher pass' (but was more likely to be 'a Darren Fletcher miscontrol') and coolly lifted the ball over the advancing tender.

Then Wayne Roonaldo added a second shortly after the half-time show when he hammered the ball so hard that goaltender Thomas Sorensen dived out the way to avoid being hurt.

It was a good win, but clearly, it was a good time to kick against the Aston Holiday Homes. Most of their starting roster had to miss the game as they had to attend their chalets on the south coast ahead of the Christmas period. And the ones that did actually play were busy trying to work out what time they needed to put the turkey in the oven on Christmas Day if they have to feed 45 guests by 2 pm.

December 18 – Sir Fergie sees his franchise lose again

Sir Fergie admitted yesterday that he is a London Arsenals fan – and promptly saw his new franchise pick up a loss against their local rivals, the London Chelseas.

Arjen Robben and Ashley Cole kicked the scores as the London Chelseas won zip-two at the Hi Berry Ballpark, leaving Manchester a further game off the pace, while the Arsenals are looking anxiously over their shoulders, seeing Sunderland wheezing into view.

But there was more drama off the gridiron than on it in a game that will be remembered as the battle of the toys and prams. Arsenals' head coach Arsene Wenger said that Michael Essien should have been ejected for using an elbow on female left cornerback Lauren.

London Chelseas' Russian coach Jose Mourinho retorted: 'Yeah well, Phil Senderos should have been ejected twice for red piece-of-paper tackles on Robben and Drogba.'

Wenger, with the calmness and intelligence that people respect him for, then responded that Claude Makelelele should have been ejected three times before the game even started, just for being Claude Makelelele.

Mourinho said Thierry Henry should have been ejected before the world began 'one more time than you said'. He then stormed into the locker room, refusing to shake hands and taking his yoyo with him. He then accused the referee of being so biased that he may as well be a war reporter on Fox News.

Wenger then broke down in tears and pleaded with Mourinho to let him play with his yoyo.

Mourinho then sobbed, 'I got you a Christmas card. Why didn't you say thank you?'

 'It was because I was embarrassed that I didn't get you one,' Wenger admitted. 'I even sent Pat Rice out to the cornershop to get you one, but they had sold out. I feel so guilty.'

'Do you want to hug?' asked Mourinho.

December 19 — Schmeichel: Who'd date a Manchester kicker?

Peter Schmeichel has insisted he would never date a Manchester kicker as they have no personalities.

Schmeichel, our second-best ever goaltender after Tim Howard, revealed he would only ever go out with Wayne Roonaldo, while Ferdinand Rio is too selfish to be a good lover.

He said the only thing they are interested in now is who has the biggest diamonds. In all soccer, I reckon Ferdinand Rio must have the biggest diamond.

He said: 'Today's team lacks personality. They certainly had that in Roy Keano. The only one with that kind of personality today is Wayne Roonaldo.

'I'm thinking about guys who could be forward with me. Roonaldo? No chance. Park? No chance. Rio? No chance. Rio has lost my respect because he only thinks about himself.'

I should point out that I was paraphrasing as I only got a brief look at the story about him, so I might have slightly misunderstood some parts.

December 20 — Birmingham Bullets 1–3 Manchester

Manchester eased into the semi-Championship game of the Carl Ing Tribute Cup after brushing aside the Birmingham Bullets.

Sir Fergie again decided to select a very strong roster, with Cristiano Roonaldo playing the whole game, while Wayne kicked for 45 minutes. Ferdinand Rio was left on the sidelines, meaning our defense was much stronger than usual.

Lewis Saha was the hero, grabbing two scores. His first was a typical Rude-type score, knocking the ball into the scoring zone from under a yard after Cristiano Roonaldo left the cornerback for dead (which is something I last saw done by OJ Simpson).

His second was far better. Gary Neville showed what the British Broadcasting Company's website called 'substantial energy and vision' (which sounds like it comes from a Scientology bible or something) and Saha fired a vicious kick into the roof of the net.

Minutes earlier, a Bullets kicker had tried an identical move, with identical results, except you should delete the part about 'roof of the net' and substitute it with 'roof of a Toyota Corolla in the car park'.

It is a mystery why Sir Fergie never used Saha more often earlier in the series. If he had been on the roster, then Manchester would still be in the Euro Series. Fact. But then there are far more pressing reasons to hate Sir Fergie than that.

In between Saha's strikes, Park Ji-Sung made his first significant contribution to Manchester – other than extending the opening hours of his Megastore by two hours – by kicking his first score. Swapping balls with Saha (which sounds pretty painful), he launched the ball past the Bullets' dyslexic goaltender Maik Taylor.

It's been a difficult series for the Birmingham Bullets so far and this won't have helped. Playing basketball Monday evenings, they are 10th of 11 franchises and then they return to soccer on Saturdays and Tuesdays and are 19th of 20 in the EPL.

However, being a basketball team, the one thing they have is height and 7'2" middleman/guard Jiri Jarosik did grab one score with a head-kick that would have impressed Peter Crouch. But then I imagine coming from Macclesfield, he's already pretty easy to impress. 'Ooh look, a flying plane!'

December 21 — Rugby tries to become popular

Soccer in Manchester is being overtaken by rugby, according to some fat dude.

The GM of the Sale Homoerotic Egg-Chasing Society (TM)

Niels de Vos believes that rugby is now far more popular than soccer around Manchester as his franchise are going to qualify for the next stages of their Euro Series. Plus soccer fans are getting frustrated at Sir Fergie's incompetence.

He claims that Sale have sold out their Christmas game in record time – to be held at Edgeley Park, their 350-capacity all-seater stadium. It might be true, but you can't compare it to soccer. I understand girl-scouts were going door-to-door selling rugby tickets for charity, so of course they were going to sell them quickly.

I think it can all be explained very easily. The rise in the interest in rugby around Manchester is simply due to the recent opening of two private boarding schools in the area and the release of 250 men currently in jail for GBH, for the holiday period.

Anyway, how can there be a rugby Euro Series? Only six nations even know the rules of rugby and only three of them are in Europe! Next the rugby weirdos will have a pennant just in their own country and call it the World Series or something.

December 22 – Sir Fergie plays the numbers game

Confusion reigns at the Nike Trafford Ballpark as Sir Fergie tears Manchester apart.

The repercussions of the exit from the Euro Series – a pennant that even a franchise like the Glasgow Rule Britannias managed to remain in – and people are laying the blame at various different places.

Sir Charlton, the Manchester deputy GM, fumed that the kickers were not giving 100% the whole time. Meanwhile, former Buccs ace Phil Neville insisted his brother Gary never gave less than 110%, which is as impressive in effort as it is unimpressive in math.

Meanwhile, the father of Manchester awesome-offenser Lewis Saha claims his son has only been able to give 65% so far, due to the bad injuries, poor coaching and French state education system. If he had only tried 35% harder this series, he would have grabbed 1.05 more scores. Maybe then we'd have only lost 4–2.05 to the Middle Borough.

But here's where I think things have gone wrong. Sir Fergie has insisted that his kickers give nothing less than 200%. It's no wonder they all looked so tired against the Ben Fica VIII . . . they had all been burning themselves out in every game trying so hard. Asking them to give 200% each game is a bit like getting higher than an A grade in an exam. I mean, they'd have to invent a new grade, like A* or something and that's just stupid.

If he just allowed his kickers to relax, I'm sure we'd do much better. Not only are they exhausted, but they are also terrified of being given the hairdresser treatment from Sir Fergie. After all, what sane man would want a hairstyle like David Beckham?

On a separate issue, you have to wonder how bad Darren Fletcher actually is if this is him at 200%!

December 23 – Manchester to sneak kicker through immigration

Manchester look set to break trade rules by drafting Nemanja Vidic.

A trade embargo was put in place in September and no more kicker moves were allowed, but Manchester are hoping to slip one more kicker on to the roster and to claim he was there all along.

Vidic is a tall, bulky defenseman, so quite how they are going to smuggle him into the Nike Trafford Ballpark in a Samsonite suitcase, I've got no idea. I understand he is quite dirty – partly because he got ejected from his national roster's last World Cup Series divisional round clash and partly because I hear his national franchise is nicknamed S&M.

One thing I'll give Vidic is that he is pretty smart. He has watched a few Manchester ballgames on his VCR and knows exactly what the problem is – Ferdinand Rio.

He said: 'They do have problems in defense, to say the least. And the most problematic area is their centre zone, from where

their opponents score much too often.' Sign him up Sir Fergie –
he can be our defensive co-ordinator.

December 25 – Merry Christmas, Manchester fans

Let's hope that the kickers are having a relaxing one and are
ready for their ballgame tomorrow. I'm sure new score-kicking
hero Lewis Sant-ha will give us plenty of presents against the
Western Bromwiches.

They put on a Christmas play yesterday to entertain the
locals and all the kickers dressed up in festive gear. I have
managed to get hold of a cast list for the show and it sounds
great.

Gary Neville dressed up as Santa, with Paul Scholes as an elf.
They didn't have an elf costume, but I don't suppose anyone
really noticed.

The reindeer were:
Dasher – Ryan Giggs
Dancer – Ji-Sung Park
Prancer – Cristiano Roonaldo
Vixen – Keiron Richardson
Comet – Lewis Saha
Cupid – Rude Nistelrooy
Donner (Kebab) – Wayne Roonaldo
Blitz 'Em – The return of Roy Keano
Rudolph – Sir Fergie (well he had the red nose for it)

So today, I only hope Sir Fergie doesn't hog the eggnog and
turn his face an even more vivid shade of puce. The kickers
would hate that – when Sir Fergie has too much eggnog, you're
either his best buddy or he wants to fight you and it's
impossible to tell which.

Happy holidays to all and I hope you all find someone nice
to kiss under the Mistelrooy (if that isn't too disturbing an
image).

December 26 — Manchester 3–0 Western Bromwiches

Manchester reached the 10-game unbeatable streak mark in the EPL after dominating the Western Bromwiches Monday.

We ravaged them as if they were the leftover turkey from Christmas Day and indeed, the Bromwiches did look a lot like turkeys for much of the game at the Nike Trafford Ballpark. Our passing was as crisp as a roast potato, while Keiron Richardson and Alan Smith looked a lot like pigs in blankets on the sidelines.

Today in Britain was a public holiday called Boxing Day and if this game was a boxing match, then the referee would have stopped it after three rounds, the public would have rioted as they paid 700 English dollars a ticket for eight minutes action, the promoters would run off with all the money and be lighting cigars with 100 English dollar-bills until the mob caught up with them and threw them into the River Thames with shoes made of the same material that Wayne Roonaldo's head is made out of.

Oh yes, the game. Paul Scholes proved that he is indeed a Christmas elf as he got the go-ahead score for Manchester at third-time. Ferdinand Rio jinked down the sideline with his samba skills and dragged the ball back for Johnny-on-the-spot Scholes to slam in.

Rio then turned from assister to scorer as he multiplied the score-advantage by two. Ryan Giggs swung over a corner-center and Rio apparently leapt like a cricketer in *Strictly Come Dancing* to head-kick his second score in as many games.

Incidentally, why do people talk about Brazilian kickers having samba skills? No one says a mega-American super-legend like Brian McBride plays with line-dancing ability. Although McBride is so old that he hardly moves outside a tiny square, so that might be quite apt.

Rude Nistelrooy made it three in the second period as he ran on to Alan Smith's center and fired an unstoppable kick past Bromwiches goaltender Tzozmazsz Kzuzszczazk (pronounced Tom's Cassocks).

It was the Bromwiches ninth road game without picking up a win and they now face the long freeway drive north to Western Bromwich.

December 27 — Wayne is a muss!

Wayne Roonaldo has admitted that he is terrified of horror films.

The Manchester star insisted that, while the prospect of facing the London Arsenals, Chelseas or Brazilian Waxes is no problem, he jumps out of his seat when watching a scary movie on cable.

It turns out a lot of Manchester kickers also have peculiar phobias, so here is a list of what they are scared of:

Ferdinand Rio – jumping
Ji-Sung Park – a market depression
Paul Scholes – burgundy sweaters
Cristiano Roonaldo – celibacy
Darren Fletcher – the soccer ball
Sir Fergie – Kaliber

December 28 — Birmingham Bullets 2–2 Manchester

What a humiliation! Manchester fell five wins behind the London Chelseas after being held to a two-to-two tie with the basketball team the Birmingham Bullets.

It is the first time this series that we have failed to get the win over a non-soccer side and it shows just how far Manchester are behind the top franchises in the division. I think too much boxing for our kickers on 'Boxing Day' is to blame as we looked punch-drunk for most of the game.

It was Olympic clay pigeon shooting entrant Walter 'The Rifle' Pandiani who got the parallel score with 12 minutes remaining, knocking the ball into the score-zone after Ferdinand Rio had dawdled, stumbled and practiced his dancing footwork inside the 18-yard zone.

Yet it had all looked so good for Manchester after Rude Nistelrooy got the go-ahead score from our first drive with just five minutes on the clock. From his standard distance (i.e. close enough to blow the ball over the score-line), he slid the ball home from Keiron Richardson's center.

Yet the Bullets, the second worst franchise in the EPL (and being foreign, Sunderland hardly count as an EPL franchise), managed to fight back soon afterwards. Jamie Clapham, named after his hometown in London not far from the Nike Trafford Ballpark, hit a kick so hard that it melted the ball and the liquid seeped under Eddie Vandersar.

Luckily we have Wayne Roonaldo and he put us back in front, shortly after the half-time Gatorade. When Nistelrooy missed controlling the ball completely – only to claim that he 'dummied' the ball – Roonaldo was on hand to finish with his left foot, the first time he has used his left foot since his last ejection for a dangerous tackle.

But the Rifle, who had just got back from a Boxing Day hunt with his posh friends, grabbed a score three minutes after being used as a replacement and we had to share the points, meaning we got $1\frac{1}{2}$ each.

We have two tough games coming up in the next week and quite frankly, if Sir Fergie is going to keep messing around, I can't see how we can win them. I assume he's messing around – why else would Darren Fletcher be on the roster at all?

One week ago, with all our top kickers cut, we shot past the Bullets in the Carl Ing Tribute Cup, but with our 'stars' back, we could only tie. Personally, I would say that our top kickers are actually Rossi, Jones, Howard etc. who can't get a kick normally. I'm sure Sir Phelan knows all this already. Come on Sir Fergie . . . step aside and give us a chance of winning!

December 29 – Liverpool Reds in crisis mode

Manchester are not the only franchise in a crisis at the moment.

Liverpool Reds fans are calling for head coach Rafa Benitez to be fired after his franchise conceded an embarrassing score against local rivals the Everton Stickies – although they will probably only be rivals for five more months as the Stickies are likely to be demoted to the Scottish League this series.

Fans are furious with the roster, calling them boring and predictable after they won again, leaving them with a win-streak extending to nine games. At least Manchester has exciting games, where you are never sure what will happen, be it a win, loss or a tie with a basketball franchise.

But after their defense had not let in a score for 12.5 hours, they let 'offenser' James Beattie grab a score – only the Stickies' tenth in 19 games, leaving the Reds on the brink of humiliation. No one concedes a score against the Stickies, not Manchester, not even the London Arsenals, who have the generousest defense amongst the Big Six franchises.

Fans want Benitez out. I wonder if they'll take Sir Fergie instead?

December 30 – Stop booing Cristiano, he's getting upset

Sir Fergie has called on opposing fans to stop jeering Cristiano Roonaldo, as it is making him upset.

The British wideout is hated by home crowds as they think he spends more time on the floor than an Olympic gymnast – and indeed the 13-year-old girls in the US squad seem to have substantially more strength than Roonaldo.

But Sir Fergie is worried that the constant booing is getting to Roonaldo, who came off the gridiron for the Birmingham Bullets game in tears, shrieking: 'Why do they hate me? What have I done? I'm a nice person! Yesterday, I put 20p in the RNLI box on the counter of my local Claire's Accessories.'

Luckily, we are playing the Boltonians at the Nike Trafford Ballpark tomorrow, then making the short journey to the London Arsenals for the biggest game of the series so far.

The Arsenals' Hi Berry Stadium is a dual-purpose building, also housing a library, which holds books on moaning, sulking and selective blindness. In fact, the stewards are also the librarians and if anyone makes any noise, they shush them or kick them out, so at least there will be no jeering there.

The only problem will be that if Eddie Vandersar doesn't have much to do, the darkness and silence could send him off to sleep.

December 31 — Manchester 4—1 Boltonians

Manchester gave Old Man Fergie a 64th birthday to remember as we ran riot, beating the Boltonians four to one at the Nike Trafford Ballpark.

The Manchester head coach had a soccer party to celebrate, where he invited all his favorite kickers – and because it was only his favorites, he cut Rude Nistelrooy. After the soccer party, everyone went swimming and then had a trip to a Wendy's with a special playhouse.

The game was one of our best kicking displays of the series as we dominated the franchise that was only three spots behind us. It was especially satisfying as the Boltonians had had a week off after someone caught their Argentinia 'headmaster' Sam Allardyce coming out of the under-gridiron heating room at their stadium with a screwdriver, a pair of garden shears and a giant bag of ice.

To be fair, although we kicked well, the Boltonians helped us as much as possible, with hall monitor Bruno Ngotty grabbing a negative score early on. Keiron Richardson's center was heading for Lewis Saha, but Ngotty showed his predatory instincts, getting there first to send it past his own goaltender.

Yet like all public schoolboys, the Boltonians are always happiest with their backs against the wall and they fought back well, against the run of the soccerball. JJ Okocha's long throw zinged around the red zone like a pinball and 42-year-old Gary Speed was the Pinball Wizard (with such a supple wrist – again like most public schoolboys), head-kicking it home.

But the Boltonians self-destructed once again as Saha raced on to Ben Tal Haim's overhead-head-kick and slid the ball into the score-zone.

After that, Cristiano Roonaldo remembered that once, he used to be a soccer player too and surged into action. He knocked two times on the metalwork and then grabbed two scores following a succession of mazy runs that left the defensemen so dizzy that they actually had canaries flying around their heads.

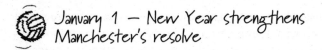

January 1 — New Year strengthens Manchester's resolve

Happy New Year everyone. It's a brand-new start in 2006 and a chance for Manchester to finally end their pennant drought after another victory-less year.

My New Year's resolution is to be nicer to Darren Fletcher, but I don't know how long it will last. I mean, I have chosen something really difficult. Not like Pop who has resolved to stay out of McDonald's for a whole week.

I managed to find a list of what the Manchester players are doing for their New Year's resolutions:

Sir Fergie – To put all the best kickers on to the roster, including Lewis Saha, at all times

Darren Fletcher – Giving up mediocrity (oops, I said I wasn't going to be mean)

Ji-Sung Park – To cut overheads, allowing a greater profit return while saving substantially on running costs

Wayne Roonaldo – To continue his community work with older people

Alan Smith – To become the new Roy Keano. I understand he has already slagged off half the Manchester roster, so it's a good start

Wes Brown – To look less like the little orphan Annie

January 3 — The battle for the first losers' spot

Manchester are preparing for their biggest game of the series – the local derby against the London Arsenals.

It's a game we desperately need to win as we bid to finish in the first losers' spot in the EPL and it will be a battle between our two franchises and the Liverpool Reds, who seem to have slipped from the best team in Europe to the third best team in England.

The Arsenals seem to have struck upon the best way to get the win over us. Pascal Cygan reckons that Wayne Roonaldo's one weakness is his brain (which ignores his other weakness for women who don't have their own teeth). Cygan reckons Roonaldo will be ejected tonight and we will end up with a loss because of it.

Well, I don't agree. Even if we do lose him, we still have Darren Fletcher and Jono Shea, who the newspaper the London *Times* compared to Keano and Robson. Unfortunately, it was Kevin Keen and Robson from Robson and Jerome.

It's going to be a big one! When we kicked against them last series, one of their players threw pizza at our roster and covered Sir Fergie in soup. Wayne Roonaldo was furious with it, as he couldn't believe there was food there that he couldn't eat. And Sir Fergie wouldn't let him lick him.

January 4 — London Arsenals 0–0 Manchester

Manchester held on to get a magnificent tie against the London Arsenals at the Hi Berry Stadium.

We were under the cosh for much of the game against a franchise that has finished with a better win-record for the last two series, but we dug in to guarantee we didn't pick up a loss.

In past series, this has been the fightingest ballgame around, yet this one was a bit disappointing. Wayne

Roonaldo pushed some Arsenals kicker into the sponsorship logos – and Roonaldo is such a good professional, that he managed to secure payment for it first.

On the other side, the London Arsenals female cornerback Lauren proved she is able to mix it with the men with a tackle of such ferocity on Cristiano Roonaldo that the Manchester kicker actually landed just outside the Nike Trafford Ballpark, almost six miles down the road.

On the gridiron, we were desperately holding on as Ferdinand Rio and Wes Brown made vital interceptions to stop certain scores, while according to one report, Eddie Vandersar stopped a rasper from Robert Pires, but quite frankly, I have no idea what that actually means. It sounds filthy.

It's not a bad result – tying with a franchise that has traditionally been much better than us is a good end-score – but I can't help feeling we could have burgled them. If only Sir Fergie had kept our recent top point-scorer Lewis Saha on the roster, instead of replacing him with Rude Nistelrooy, who last night couldn't hit an elephant's behind with a cello, let alone anything smaller.

And it could have been worse – Thierry Henry, one of the best kickers in the world, could have been playing for the London Arsenals.

January 5 – Sir Fergie comes up with new gameplan

Sir Fergie has discovered another way of winning the EPL. He is going to nobble the entire London Chelseas roster!

The Manchester head coach's first idea was to rely on his expertise – give them all haircuts, but 'accidentally' nip their ears with the scissors. But instead, he hinted that he was going to start a malaria outbreak in the Chelseas' locker room.

Dr Mary Galinski, the head of Malaria Foundation International (MFI), who are attempting to control the disease in the developing world by improving the range of

MDF fitted kitchen facilities, was furious with Sir Fergie's suggestion.

She said: 'My first reaction when I heard it was: "Oh my God! He may as well have said: 'Wouldn't it be great if a tsunami hit where Chelsea are playing?'"'

Maybe she should be our head coach! That's a much better idea than Sir Fergie's!

January 6 — It's Manchester for Evra

Manchester are set to complete their January revamp of their defensive line by drafting cornerback Patricia Evra.

Evra will become Manchester's first ever lady kicker when she makes the trip to the Nike Trafford Ballpark next week, although a number of people have claimed that Darren Fletcher runs like a girl.

The defensewoman is one of the rare breed of players that has been kicking on her national roster – the nation of Monaco – but is not connected to any franchise, so she should be the bargain of the year so far.

She will stand in for Gabriel Heinze, while the Argentinia cornerback is on the Injured Reserve, and then Evra will sit on the sidelines alongside Quinton Fortune and all the other sub-standard kickers that Sir Fergie has drafted.

She is the second trade of the week, after Nemanja Vidic joined from the Moscow Chelseas, which seems like a real steal.

It appears that there is some kind of trade amnesty from the Soccer Association, where they are turning a blind eye to deals done throughout January, despite the fact that they are not actually allowed.

January 8 — Burton Albinos 0—0 Manchester

Manchester secured a superb tie against the Burton Albinos in their SA Super Bowl third stage play-off game.

It means that we will now get a lucrative rematch, which will help pay off the Manchester debt that everyone seems to be talking about so much. The Albinos' Pirelli Stadium was full for the game today, so I'm sure the Nike Trafford Ballpark will be a sell-out as well.

I assume that Burton is a coastal town in Britain, as the game seemed to be played on a beach, such was the amount of sand on the gridiron. And because they were having a trip to the seaside, Sir Fergie took all his youngsters along, meaning a starting spot on the roster for Richie Jones, who even brought his bucket and spade and kicked the entire 90 minutes in his Speedos.

All in all, I think it was a good result for Manchester, especially considering we picked up a loss against the Albinos in November. At least this time we managed to go one better and tie.

Not that we didn't have a great deal of luck. The Burton Albinos had two head-kicks stopped on the score-line, one from Darren Stride and one from Draco Malfoy from Harry Potter.

The Albinos also thought they should have got a 12-yard kick-ball punishment after Spanish defenseman Gerard Pique caught the soccerball in the red zone and rolled it out to the cornerback. But the referee correctly remembered rule 13.2a (sub-section III) of the Soccer Association playbook that states that no 12-yard kick-ball punishments should be awarded against Manchester at any period.

Our best score chance came in the last seconds of the game, after Sir Fergie had called a time-out to bring on the Roonaldo brothers as replacements. Jones hit a ferocious air-kick, which the Albinos goaltender dived out of the way of, but his red eyes saw the ball on to his foot and he kicked it away.

So we're still in the SA Super Bowl and have a money-spinning game against the Albinos in nine days' time. All in all, a pretty good day for Manchester. And Sir Fergie picked Lewis Saha ahead of Rude Nistelrooy, so things are looking up for us.

January 9 — Tough new life for Keano

Roy Keane has discovered that the grass isn't always greener on the other side after his debut for the Glasgow Ireland-Greens ended in humilation.

The Scotchland champions were beaten by minor league franchise the Clyde Andbonnies, who Manchester destroyed six-zip in a pre-series game, and who were coached last series by Ronald McDonald (seriously!).

Keano was livid, saying: 'It was terrible. The defensemen were terrible, the middlemen non-existent and the offensers seemed completely disinterested.' He also said the head coach seemed to be completely incompetent.

He then went on to say that he's just relieved he's left all that behind now and is at a franchise that is top of their pennant division.

January 10 — Albinos gone for a Burton

Manchester can consider themselves lucky to have got a tie with the Burton Albinos on Sunday. But at least we got a relatively easy play-off game. It certainly could have been much worse.

We could have been make to kick against the Stour Bridges, who are in the Midlands Alliance League, which must be very strong as it's sponsored by a worldwide banking corporation. It will probably change its name to the HSBC Alliance League next series.

The Bridges beat the Albinos four-to-one! Imagine how many they would have scored against Manchester, who were lucky to escape with zip-zip intact!

I wonder if the HSBC Alliance League is a breakaway division above the EPL Divisional League where all the very top franchises go.

Another gameday and another fine result as Manchester's resurgence continues. This time we held on for a one-to-one tie at the Blackburn Pyros to force a rematch in the Carl Ing Tribute Cup semi-Championship game.

We will now face the Pyros again in two weeks' time to decide who goes on to meet the Wigan Warriors in the final of the competition, which will be played at a half-finished Wembley Stadium in February.

It was a great performance by Manchester to tie with the Pyros on the road, having previously suffered a loss to them in our hometown game. It is never easy going to play in the Blackburn Prison Institution, where Cristiano Roonaldo looked slightly nervous.

And it looks even better when you consider Sir Fergie is starting to show signs of old age. He told everyone during the day, that he would be using his back-up kickers, but then named his strongest possible roster (with the exception of Darren Fletcher obviously).

And for five minutes, we even had a winning scoreline after a terrific Lewis Saha score. He seems to be repaying our faith after Sir Fergie read my cries for him to be included at the expense of Rude Nistelrooy. Now if only Sir Fergie could obey my other petition and get himself fired, everyone would be happier.

Ryan Giggs made the kind of run through the middle that Pop tells me he used to do on a regular basis, and then slipped in Saha, who rifled the soccerball past American super-stopper Brad Friedel, who is currently serving five years for trying to sneak into Britain without the proper paperwork.

But Morten Gamst Pedersen, who kicked two scores at the Nike Trafford Ballpark earlier in the series, added another one straight afterwards to give the Pyros a parallel score. He ran on to a long ball and rifled his kick into the top corner with the accuracy of Charlton Heston at an NRA meeting.

After that, we held solid to grab a rematch, although

there was a bit of a scrap when Alan Smith scythed down Robbie Savage and the Pyros middleman got offended when the referee congratulated Smith and then gave him tips on how he could have caused more damage with his tackle.

January 12 — Sir Fergie grovels to Super Malcolm

Great news. Sir Fergie has realized that he is close to losing his job at Manchester.

The head coach has been under pressure in recent months after we were dumped out of the Euro Series and, despite the upturn of form that has seen us gain creditable ties with the Burton Albinos and Blackburn Pyros, Sir Fergie has decided to kiss the feet of Super Malcolm Glazer.

Sir Fergie labeled the Glaz-meister and his triplets 'excellent' and said they have never failed to support the franchise since they bought it. He also said that Super Malcolm has a nice car and takes extremely good care of his beard.

This must mean that Sir Fergie has realized he is close to getting cut and is desperately trying to build bridges. And I only mentioned him leaving on my website yesterday. Maybe the Glaz-meister reads it! Now that would be awesome! If you do read the site, Malc-meister, can you get me tickets for a Manchester game sometime?

January 13 — Manchester minor league side 3–1 Manchester

Manchester's starting roster suffered a humiliation after picking up an embarrassing three-to-one loss to the minor league kickers.

We had been in terrific form recently, with a win-or-tie streak stretching to 11 games, but the kickers that Sir Fergie picks were easily beaten by the ones he doesn't. I thought it was bad when we only tied with them earlier in the series, but this is too much to bear!

Trevor Sinclair, who has to supplement his meagre minor league income by inventing environmentally friendly cars, got the first score, spinning on a nickel to fire past Eddie Vandersar.

Darius Vassell multiplied the scoreline by two shortly afterwards as he ran on to a through-kick, which Michael Silvester should have cleared, but decided instead to do his impression of a man desperately trying to get out of some quicksand (which is a pretty good metaphor for his position at Manchester this series).

And as if things couldn't get any worse, Cristiano Roonaldo was ejected for a lunge at former starting kicker Andy-Andrew Cole that was so wild that you can normally only see them on safari in Africa.

Sir Fergie had made the mystifying decision to remove form-offenser Lewis Saha and bring back Rude Nistelrooy and the Hollandish man did pull one score back. He showed good strength to hold off 4' 3" defenseman Sun Jihai and found that same nickel Sinclair used to spin on and beat former Britain goaltender David James.

Manchester pushed forward looking for the parallel score, but the minor leaguers took advantage and Robbie Fowler, who was a top kicker until he was forced to seek help for an addiction to sniffing paint, made it three at a time when the referee's finger was already on the final buzzer.

January 14 — Where now for Manchester?

Yesterday's defeat at the hands of the minor league franchise was one of the worst games I can remember in the long time that I have been a Manchester fan.

But I've had some time to think about it now and maybe it's not as bad as I originally thought. I think there are quite a few positives that we can take from the game.

First and foremost, at least it was only an exhibition game that we lost, so it won't harm our hopes of finishing in second spot in the EPL standings.

And secondly, it shows that Manchester has a huge roster

of hungry, talented kickers. If they could be given a shot at the major leagues, they would be given enough money to buy food and wouldn't be hungry any more, which can only make them better kickers.

We just need a coach that recognizes the potential of these kickers, who have all been drafted by Manchester at some stage, only to be cast aside.

It could be getting even worse for the beleaguered Manchester coach after it was announced that the SA would be investigating claims of a conversation between Sir Fergie and the referee, but I think it will be fine.

Sir Fergie is believed to have offered referee Steve Bennett a lift home in a police car (a Ford Escort to be precise) to avoid all the traffic around the ground, but Bennett appears to have reported him – presumably for bribing one of the officials. As they say around the Nike Trafford Ballpark, 'it never rains, it pours', but I think they mean it literally, not metaphorically.

January 15 – I'm coming to the Nike Trafford Ballpark!

OH! MY! GOD!

I have the givingest Pop in the world! As a surprise 'pre-birthday' present, Pop has just told me that he has got us tickets for the big Manchester v Liverpool Reds game in Round 24 of the EPL series!

We are leaving for Britain in less than a week for the big game. Pop said he didn't want to tell me any earlier as I wouldn't be able to concentrate on schoolwork if he did. Apparently, I've got permission to miss one day of school to be away, as long as I write about my trip on the plane ride and bring the teacher some English muffins – they're bound to be better from England.

I'm so excited I could explode. Pop looks like he could explode too, but that's because of the four Big Macs he has just eaten.

January 16 — Too much information on Scholes

Paul Scholes is suffering from a serious sight condition that's troubling the medical staff at the Nike Trafford Ballpark.

To be honest, I hadn't even noticed he wasn't on the roster. When he hadn't kicked a score recently, I just assumed his form had slumped again.

Scholes has been on the sidelines for the last five games due to an eye condition that, depending upon where you read it, varies from slightly blurred vision to going blind.

I can see why it's baffling doctors – what could possibly cause him to go blind, have stunted growth and have hairy palms? It's a real mystery.

January 17 — Rude and Roonaldo fight it out

Fellow Manchester rosterers Rude Nistelrooy and Cristiano Roonaldo have been involved in a fight at the franchise's practice ground.

The pair had to be pulled apart and were sent to the principal's office after a scrap regarding Roonaldo's ejection from the exhibition clash against the minor league roster on Saturday.

I don't imagine the fight was that impressive. Reports claim that at the start, both kickers flung themselves to the ground despite minimal contact between the two. It is believed that Roonaldo came out the better of the two. He managed to pull out a bit of Rude's hair and only suffered mild grazing from a handbag in return.

So another bad day for Manchester. The only bright spot of the day is that Sir Fergie reckons we'll earn 0.75 million English dollars from our SA Super Bowl clash with the Burton Albinos. Just another 539.25 million to go and we'll be out of debt! Go Buccs!

We're helping out with our two tickets to Sunday's game. Pop was right, I really haven't been able to think about anything at school this week. Yesterday, the math teacher

asked me what seven multiplied by six is and I answered
'Giuseppe Rossi'.

I can't wait to see what the Nike Trafford Ballpark looks
like. The Tampa Bay Buccaneers Stadium has a giant pirate
ship, which fires cannons when we score. I wonder what
Manchester has like that. Perhaps whenever Wayne
Roonaldo scores, a giant pie appears from one end of the
stadium.

January 18 — Manchester 5–0 Burton Albinos

Manchester stormed into the next phase of the SA Super
Bowl with a five-zip rout of the Burton Albinos.

Awesome offenser Giuseppe Rossi grabbed two scores as
Mancheser ensured that their score-differential got a boost,
which could come in useful later in the competition. I
always thought that Rossi was American, but it turns out
he's actually Italian–American, which explains why he is
such a good hitman.

Lewis Saha slid the soccerball into the score-zone after just
seven minutes to put Manchester in front, then Rossi,
nicknamed Corleone, leapt high to head-kick the second
score, although his high leap was still knee-height for the
Albinos' defensemen.

Keiron Richardson has clearly found the level that he is
suited to, as he added a third, before Ryan Giggs got a part
of the action as he aims to become only the third kicker in
history to have five winners' rings, which will make him
look a little like BA Baracus, but what can you do about
that?

Rossi also had time to pay tribute to his brothers Sonny
and Fredo before adding a fifth score inside the two-minute
warning. Wayne Roonaldo had better watch out . . . he has
a super-Italian-American after his place. And Wayne better
not be mean to him or he'll wake up to find Rude
Nistelrooy's head in his bed.

Afterwards, Sir Fergie was happy, claiming, 'We could
have got more, but we didn't want to humiliate anyone.'

Although he failed to mention that the majority of the Manchester roster felt humiliated after the zip-zip tie with the Albinos last week.

I hope we haven't used up all our kick-scores ahead of our visit. We leave on Friday and the last thing I want is to see a zip-zip tie.

January 19 – Manchester full of vermin!

The Nike Trafford Ballpark could be infested with mice, according to some reports today.

Several Burton Albinos players claimed they saw a mouse at the stadium, close to the soccerers' tunnel, but the franchise were quick to play down the problem, suggesting the Albinos' red eyes were simply mistaken.

But they did admit they occasionally have mice in the stadium. I understand Manchester had originally tried putting traps down to catch the mice, but had to rethink when Wayne Roonaldo kept getting caught in them when he tried to steal the cheese.

Maybe this is the gimmick that they have at the Ballpark. Perhaps the Glaz-meister is trying to turn it into a zoo. They already have a horse and several donkeys on the roster.

Anyway, I'm all packed and ready to come over. We leave tomorrow morning. All I need to buy when I'm in Britain is a Manchester jersey and a humane mousetrap that won't hurt Wayne.

January 20 – I'm above cloud nine!

I was so excited on the plane over to London that I could barely eat anything. Although to be fair, none of the other passengers seemed to be able to stomach the food either.

There was a soccer film on the plane called 'Goal' although I think 'Score!' would have been a better name for it – I don't think I've ever seen the word 'goal' used in a soccer sense. It was about this South American kid who realizes his dream of kicking for the Newcastle Stripers.

It was so unrealistic. What kind of talented soccerer from the streets of Argentinia dreams of growing up to kick for a franchise in the lower reaches of the EPL, who play in a cold, wet, dreary place? Very silly film, but it got me even more excited about the game on Sunday.

I have spent my time on the flight making a list of places in London that I really want to see – the most important sites in the city . . . the London Eye, the David Beckham school of elocution and Sir Fergie's hairdressing college.

After a flight that seemed to last for weeks, we landed at London Gatwick airport, which isn't actually anywhere near London. I hope the Nike Trafford Ballpark isn't as far out as that!

January 21 – I'm in London!

I'm here and London is an incredible place. Everything is really old and small – the buildings, the cars, even the tramps.

The London Eye was really good, although apparently, it was just too hazy out to see Manchester's stadium. From up there, we did get to see Wembley Stadium though, which looks amazing considering it is 90 years old! Its centerpiece is a huge arch, which is so big, the guide said, that even the fattest kid in my class could limbo underneath it!

We then walked past Big Ben, which was cool, Westminster Abbey, which was dirty and Downing Street, which was surrounded by so many policemen and TV chefs holding petitions that I could hardly see it.

We then went up towards Piccadilly Circus, which I had been told is like Times Square's little brother. Well, it was garbage. The only connection between the two is that they both have lots of lights and are full of foreigners. I can only assume it is the runt of the Square litter, the one that the parents wanted nothing to do with. The Phil Neville of City Squares, if you will.

I then found a store called 'Soccerscene' and immediately

went in to buy a Manchester jersey. I opted for a red one and asked to have 'Glazer' printed on the back. The clerk looked at me strangely and asked if I liked hospital. I wasn't sure what he was talking about – I imagine Hospital must be a nickname for one of the Manchester kickers. Probably Darren Fletcher, due to the number of hospital passes he gives every game.

He did eventually give me the jersey and I will definitely wear it tomorrow, when we have tickets for the biggest game of the series – the one that could help decide whether Manchester finishes in our desired second spot in the EPL standings this year. After being a fan for ages and ages, I will finally get to visit the Nike Trafford Ballpark.

It will be the best day of my life, whatever happens.

January 22 – Manchester 0–0 Liverpool Reds

Well that was a huge letdown. I don't even know where to begin on one of the worst days of my life.

While Pop and I went to the game, Mom stayed in the center of the city and said she was going to go to Soho to see Nelson's column. I said I didn't think Nelson's column was in Soho, but she insisted the column she wanted to see was there.

We left our hotel on Mayfair extra early as we wanted to enjoy the famous pre-game entertainment that they put on at the Nike Trafford Ballpark. I wanted to get the subway to the stadium, but Pop thought it would be better getting a taxi as he could see a few more sights.

Well I reckon London cab drivers are worse than New York ones! That guy ripped us off big time. I know the ballpark is a bit out of town, but this journey took over four hours! It's lucky we left early. He must have taken us to Scotchland and back or something. Then he charged us 700 English dollars for the journey. Unbelievable!

After paying that, Pop was so short of money that he told me we had to restrict ourselves to just three shrimp sandwiches. How is that going to keep us going? And because we were a bit late, all the tailgaters had packed up and gone into the stadium.

Still, I thought, at least we'll have the cheerleaders to entertain us before the roster is announced. Well, I don't think there were any. I say I don't *think* there were as our tickets were right at the top of the North Stand at the Nike Trafford Ballpark, officially making us closer to the gridiron at the London Arsenals' stadium than Manchester's.

A few Manchester fans were shouting stuff at me, but I couldn't quite make out what they were saying. I only picked out the odd word, like 'shirt', 'Glazer' and 'scum'. Not sure what it means. I expected to feel right at home amongst the Manchester fans, but they seemed like very angry people. I suppose I'd be angry as well if it rained 300 days a year.

Then the two franchises came out – Manchester walking on to the gridiron side-by-side with Europe's top franchise. I was so far away that I could hardly work out which kicker was which. The only one I could make out was Wayne Roonaldo as I could see the vein on his neck throbbing.

Because there were no dancing girls, the fans were forced to sing just to keep themselves entertained. The Manchester fans were singing songs called, 'You are my Solskjaer', 'Hey Rude' and a great song, to the tune of 'Hey Baby', which went: 'Hey Park, Ji-Sung, I wanna kno-o-o-ow, what time does your store close tonight?' They also appeared to boo every time Rude Nistelrooy did something. I never realized he was quite as unpopular as he is.

During the first half, Manchester seemed to be playing six kickers as middle-middlemen and it meant that the soccerball was just pinballing its way around the field. To be honest, I don't remember either goaltender having to make a stop, but I was so far away from the other end, that I wouldn't have known even if they did.

Now, the last time I went to a Tampa Bay Buccs game, for the half-time show, we had Jon Bon Jovi singing a medley of his greatest hits. So what excitement would Manchester put on here?

Was Elton John going to perform 'Candle in the Wind' as a tribute to Roy Keano? Would Paul McCartney appear? No. We had a man called Arthur Albiston running a tombola stall on the gridiron. The only bright spot is that I didn't win either of the bottles of pickled onions on offer.

As the second half developed, the Liverpool Reds showed why they are the best franchise in Europe and we were really hanging on for dear life. Jibril Cisse had two golden opportunities to kick the Reds go-ahead score within 10 seconds, but Ferdinand Rio cleared the first one off the score-line and then Cisse blazed the second so far over the horizontal bar that it almost came and hit us!

As there were 67,000 people there, Pop thought it was best if we left a couple of minutes before the end or he said we'd never find a taxi anywhere, so with Manchester having had just one kick at the score-zone – Rude's weak looping effort straight into the goaltender's arms – we took off.

Just as we had left the stadium, we heard a big shout from the crowd and I assume that was just the final hooter and everyone cheered from the relief of not having to watch any more of that garbage.

I can't believe just how bad a day I've had. Eight hours in a taxi to watch us have one chance of a score in a zip-zip tie? Is that what soccer is all about?

January 23 – The end?

No way! Pop's just told me that Manchester won the game yesterday after all! It turns out that Ferdinand Rio head-kicked home the winner inside the two-minute warning and we ended up with the win! Incredible!

But that just makes my day yesterday even more disappointing. I don't understand how I could have such an awful experience going to see a franchise that I love so much and have supported for a long time.

It's not surprising that people tell me that Manchester has lots of fans that have never even been to the Nike Trafford Ballpark – I wish I was still one of them!

What this has made me realize is that I just can't follow Manchester while Sir Fergie is still in charge. It's too painful and the rollercoaster ride doesn't feature enough high bits (and the high bits are kind of the point of rollercoasters).

Following the franchise from the US, I never realized just how far behind their rivals Manchester actually are. We may have won yesterday, but it was a Bonnie and Clyde win – pure daylight robbery (although Manchester seemed to have very little daylight).

We didn't have a kick aimed at the score-zone until 82 minutes had passed and only had one corner-center in the whole game. With the current head coach in charge, we are just not going anywhere. We have a roster with a few incredibly talented kickers, some quite talented ones and one who the best thing you can say about him is that he is the best kicker at the franchise called Darren.

But under Sir Fergie, we are on a long pennant-less run and it won't end under him. Glaz-meister, please give the job to Sir Phelan or even Stuart Pearce. In fact, anyone will do, as long as he's not a hairdresser from Scotchland. Then maybe I will feel like I can watch Manchester again.

I also never realized just how little actually happens in soccer. I mean, the game lasts for 90 minutes, with hardly any interruptions and yet the only thing I remember about yesterday's game is there was lots of sideways passing and then kicking the ball off the field. Two kicks at the goaltender in a whole game? Americans wouldn't stand for it.

That's why the game hasn't taken off back home and, quite frankly, 500 million people can't be wrong. Clearly, I should have listened to them and stuck to the sports that are popular all over the world – like baseball or football.

The next time I say 'Go Buccs', it will be for Tampa Bay, not Manchester.

GLOSSARY

Manchester My beloved team! The best in the Britain league!

London Chelseas New EPL champions from Russia

London Arsenals Beat Manchester in the SA Super Bowl

Everton Stickies Qualified for the European Series

Liverpool Reds European Series winners after a 12-yard kick-ball challenge

The Boltonians From a posh Bolton private school

The Middle Borough Central London side

Tott Nam Mainly young Vietnamese players

The Aston Holiday Homes Players get a free seaside apartment in Birmingham

Charlton Addicts Team from the Outreach program

Birmingham Bullets EPL side from Alabama

Fulham Fayeds Egyptian champions

Newcastle Stripers Commercial roster whose players play in barcodes

Blackburn Pyros Northern prison franchise

Pompeii Pompeys The only ancient roster still in existence

Western Bromwiches Keiron Richardson rocks! Trade him for Sir Ferguson!

Western Hammers From the west England town of Wales

Wigan Warriors Rugby side

Sunderland National franchise from European country of Sunderland

THE BEST OF THE READERS' COMMENTS

My Manchester Buccaneers website had a comments section, especially for fellow Manchester fans to leave remarks discussing our favorite franchise. Unfortunately, some people weren't very nice, especially considering they were writing to a 12-year-old boy!

Here are the best of the readers comments . . . well, the ones that were printable anyway.

This whole site must be a joke, an Arsenal or City fan having a laugh! If it is genuine then you yanks wanna keep your mouth shut about something you clearly know NOTHING about.

You dont hear British people talking about American Football (how much padding do they wear?) or ice hockey (how much padidng do they wear?) so leave the 'Soccer' to us will ya, we dont need to break the US, we were big enough and profitable enough already, so all you yanks can go suck a puck!

For your information (please take note of this otherwise British people will continue to laugh at you) We DONT call them '12-yard goal challenge' we call them PENALTIES, or in this case a PENALTY SHOOT-OUT. A 12-yard challenge sounds more like something youd do in the pub with a rather tall glass of beer.

We DONT call it the European Series, its called the UEFA CHAMPIONS LEAGUE, again your trying to ruin our national game with your idiotic americanised terms. FOOTBALL was started around 1890, the last time Utd won the European Cup (not series) was indeed in the 60s, under a man called Sir Matt Busby, now this man is a legend in football, and some of the best players EVER seen in football history were playing then, clearly you know nothing about the history of the game.

THE WORST ONE OF THE LOT — Manchester are a northern team you SPASTIC! look on any map of the UK, Manchester and Liverpool are right near each other and are in the NORTH of ENGLAND You CANNOT refer to MUFC simply as Manchester, there are two teams from Manchester, United and City, both in the Premiership, so please from now on, its Man Utd or Manchester Utd. Saying just Manchester shows everyone how little you know about football.

Until you get these facts right, there is no way you can use the term WE. Manchester Utd do not need you as a fan, they already are one the biggest teams in Europe, so stick to your American Football and go stick your dollars up your fat butt! Published by: UnsellingStarling — 26 May 15:52

1) It's Wayne Rooney
2) It's just Arsenal
3) Wright-Phillips plays for Manchester City
4) It's Roy Keane
5) Keane is Irish, so of course he wont get in the England squad
6) ENGLAND beat USA. Not Britain.
7) Call 'your' team United, or Manchester United. Not Manchester

P.S. You're a tit
Published by: Stevie Baby — 31 May 15:02

Dude, he allready played for manu some years ago and he SUCKED! Just a couple of things ... Roy Keane cant play for the english national team, he is irish ... And wales aint a city, its a country. Last it aint called the super bowl or any of that american stuff, its only called the FA cup! 31 May 16:17
Published by: WTF?

Mate, you're a class A retard. 1. It's a cup, a league, a trophy, a competition but it isn't a series! 2. It's not the 'Charlton Addicts', it's Charlton Athletic. They're knickname is the Addicts but you don't stick it on the end of their name! 3. Winningest? Since when was that a word?
Published by: RustableClown — 03 June 11:42

I really do hope that this is a joke. I know that americans aren't the sharpest tools in the box but come on. It seems obvious to me that you people have absolutely no idea what you're talking about when it comes to Football (yes, it's called football). I'd suggest you actually read about the game from a British Football site and maybe then you'll understand just how ignorant you all appear to be. If an Englishman had just completed a hostile takeover of a yanky 'football' team i wouldn't rush to post a load of ill researched crap about a sport i don't understand. But hey, what do i know?
Published by: Giersstu — 06 June 07:37

Get your facts straight. Rooney and Ronaldo are not related. Robbie Fowler plays for Manchester CITY, which is another club entirely. There is no 'British' team, just England, Scotland, Wales and Ireland. Asia is a continent not a country. I could go on but i don't have enough time. This website is a joke.
Published by: theslime — 28 June 15:30

er ... crespo is alreddy a chelsea playa, hes on loan at milan cuz hes crap 4 chelsea. and its juan sebastian veron, ur gettin confused with anotha playa. as 4 arnesen, i wont even say how stupid u r! sum 1 else can do that!
Published by: drv wicketts — 29 June 11:29

u hav sum seriously screwed up mind u r obs deffo not a MANCHESTER UNITED fan coz wa wise u'd no mor about the ENGLISH PREMIERSHIP. do ya research betta if u fink u wona b 1 ov us tho u must be so fick to fink that vierra is a irishman bludy hell. so jus keep ur imature comments to ya self an giv sum of the real supporters some peace an quiet from the yank called glazer
Published by: andyc 142 — 20 July 11:53

'Keano, the best Manchester player to never play for England.' What the hell is this rubbish? He's Irish! Oh, and you've split your infinitive too. It should be 'never to play'. Dumb yank.
Published by: Adam Skeet — 25 July 19:32

you really are a stupid little boy, you should learn some more about man utd before writing about them
Published by: a real man utd supporter — 26 August 21:41

SEARCHES USED TO FIND THE MANCHESTER BUCCANEERS WEBSITE

The majority of people that found the Manchester Buccaneers website found it through one of the web's many search engines. Some were actually searching for it, but some were hoping to find something very different and stumbled across this instead, thanks to the wonderful way Mister Internet works.

Here is a list of just a few terms that were searched for by people who found my humble site:

frank lampard's parents
pictures of wayne rooney that your allowed
msn display picture of little britain
Mutton dressed as lamb Carol Vorderman
prawn logo
strapon spaces.msn.com
Hairdressers in Manchester
Escorts in Manchester
Beijing prostitutes OR Escorts
Cristiano Ronaldo topless
Fergie xxx

ACKNOWLEDGEMENTS

There are so many people I need to thank for helping me publish my diaries and help make Manchester into a soccer franchise that is well-known worldwide.

Firstly, special thanks to Alan, Mark, Lucinda, Jess and everyone else at Weidenfeld & Nicolson for all the hard work they have done on this project. Many thanks also to David Luxton of Luxton Harris, who has made the world of publishing seem extremely easy.

Thank you very much to my buddy Simon Dickson, who was a great help in formulating the idea for my diaries, to my family and friends, who have all been extremely supportive and helpful, and also to Ian and Rob from thepredictionsite.com, who were a great help with cheese-related puns.

I am forever indebted to the idiots that left irate and abusive comments on my website, which helped make it as popular as it is. The stupidity of the general public in Britain has been a huge help for me. And thanks to my English teacher at school for allowing me to use this diary as an assignment, instead of having to write a 300-word description of a famous painting (which is almost as fun as watching the painting dry in the first place).

And finally, thank you to the Glaz-meister, Sir Fergie, Roy Keano and the rest of the family at Manchester, whose general ineptness has been a never-ending source of inspiration for my diaries.

Roswell P. Shambling